OFFSHORE ISLANDS
OF
NOVA SCOTIA AND NEW BRUNSWICK

OFFSHORE ISLANDS

OF

NOVA SCOTIA

AND

NEW BRUNSWICK

by
Allison Mitcham
illustrated by Peter Mitcham

LANCELOT PRESS
Hantsport, Nova Scotia

To Peter, Stephanie and Inkster

my islanding companions

ISBN 0-88999-233-9

Published 1984
    Second printing November, 1984
    Third printing December 1985
LANCELOT PRESS LIMITED, Hantsport, N.S.
Office and plant situated on Highway No. 1, ½ mile east of Hantsport.

4

CONTENTS

ACKNOWLEDGEMENTS

I wish to thank the research council of the Université de Moncton for assistance given to research for this book.

* * * * * * * * *

In addition, I wish to thank the following people for information and/or moral support: Harry, Ruth, Tanya and Christian VanBuskirk, Mike Goulden, Chief and Mrs. Peter Barlow, Eric Kraus, John Harris, Robert and Geraldine Spears, Ted Clements and family, Phyllis Roy, Joseph Casey, Sr., Yvonne Chiasson, Gerald Bellefleur, Clarence Jeffrey, Ida Hagar, Doug Patterson and family, Ruth Cunningham, Stanley Young, Stanley La Pointe, Mr. and Mrs. Arnold DeMings, Clarke Perry, Steve Proctor.

INTRODUCTION

Small islands, like ships, are fascinating — and for many of the same reasons. Surrounded by water, cut off from conventional society on the mainland, life on both is strictly governed by storms and tides as well as by the unavoidable interaction of human beings confined to a limited space. On a ship as on an island it is virtually impossible to avoid close contact with the others who live there too; and so, as countless writers of sea stories have shown, this makes for a different sort of relationship between individuals. Depending on circumstances, both tolerance and hostility have a deeper hold on ships and islands than on the mainland where individuals are freer to come and go independently of their neighbors. After all, one can as easily leave some of our offshore islands in storm or fog or shifting ice as one can put out from an Ocean liner in mid Atlantic. Because of this, dramas at sea and on islands develop whereas on land the tensions causing them are more apt to be diffused.

A good example of explosive tension resulting in a dramatic series of events occurred early in the last century on Grand Manan when Mr. Wilfred Fisher, nicknamed "The Emperor of Grand Manan," took the law into his own hands because he felt his power threatened. Like the captain of a ship, he apparently demanded a sort of absolute allegiance from the islanders, an allegiance unthinkable on the mainland. Like a power-mad captain in a Melville novel, Mr. Fisher set out to demonstrate his authority, convinced that he *was* the law. (The events leading up to Mr. Fisher's actions and the outcome are discussed in the chapter on Grand Manan.)

Dramas are also triggered on both ships and islands by accidents and emergencies which on the mainland can be more easily dealt with because of access to special equipment and personnel. Fires, storms, sudden and severe illnesses, accidents — all seem more traumatic occurrences at sea than on the mainland. At the same time such events also call for the sort of hardiness and individual initiative which is less often needed on the mainland.

For these reasons, islands and ships are particularly rich sources of folklore. There is a mystique surrounding both — an aura of romance, mystery and adventure. Tales of ghosts, pirates, treasure, strange and inexplicable happenings, of heroism and disaster, hover with the persistence of sea gulls around both ships and islands.

There is a uniqueness about each boat or island. Although obviously having certain basics in common, any long-time sailor or islander would be quick to dispel a mainlander's contention that one ship or island is much like another. They are individual, manned by crews of very different sorts.

The islands represented in this book — relatively small islands off the coasts of Nova Scotia and New Brunswick — have been selected because they are so different from one another, and because each is, in its own way, so special. The islands vary in size, in racial and religious backgrounds of their inhabitants, in geographical settings, in topography, and in historical, ecological, aesthetic and commercial significance. Although all have at one time been connected with fishing, each one has other associations. Some are important as bird nesting grounds; others have so strongly grasped the imagination of visitors that they have been chosen as the settings of novels and poems; and most are associated with exceptional individuals — some internationally famous, others well-known in Atlantic Canada, and still others by and large unknown before the appearance of this book.

Finally, the connections each of these islands has with the nearby mainland are, to some extent, important here. Obviously the bond between Scatarie and Louisbourg, between Tancook and Chester, between McNutt's and Shelburne, can hardly be overlooked. There are, as well,

8

links among the islands — among the Fundy islands, for instance, and among the Northumberland Strait islands. Yet while recognizing regional similarities which certain islands share, it is nevertheless the uniqueness of each island which remains the dominant and lasting impression.

10

Chapter One

GRAND MANAN: "THE ISLAND"

"The name MANAN, of Grand and Petit Manan, is certainly of Maliseet-Passamaquoddy-Penobscot Indian origin, and means simply THE ISLAND, the prefixes having been added by the French to distinguish the two."

— W.F. Ganong
The Origin and History of the Name
Grand Manan

For the Loyalist settlers and their descendents, as for the Indians before them, Grand Manan has always been the island dominating its own archipelago as well as much of the rest of the Bay of Fundy. Whatever the difficulties of living here — and there are many (the icy water, dangerous shoals and currents surrounding the island, the fierce gales, the dense fogs, and the two-hour ferry crossing from the New Brunswick mainland) — Mananers seem almost unanimously agreed that their island is the best place in the world to live.

Part of the reason for this attitude is the success of its fisheries which are among the most flourishing in the world. The extreme coldness of the water, the high tides and dangerous eddies, the shoals and ledges, seem to provide just the environment which the fish crave.

Catches off the island have been legendary, so it is almost impossible to impress a Mananer with a fish story. He is sure to be able to top it. If you do not believe him, he may well refer you to a serious statistical report — not necessarily a contemporary one — to back him up. Here is one such account taken from *The Perley Report on the Fisheries of Grand Manan* (1850):

> The upper part of Grand Harbour . . . abounds with lobster, which during the season may be taken with a gaff, in almost any quantity . . . As many as were required for the hooker were quickly taken in this way, in two to four feet of water; the places resorted to by lobsters were easily known by the holes made by them in the flats . . .[1]

Word of such plenty has always spread quickly, and in the middle years of the last century a state of almost open war existed between the islanders and intruders, many of them the Mananers' American cousins who were keen to share the bounty. Since Grand Manan is only about six miles off the American coast and almost four times that distance from the Canadian mainland, the American intrusion was easy and Canadian protection hard to come by. Still, as Perley shows in the following excerpt from his report, the Mananers were quite prepared to defend their interests — often using rather unconventional methods:

> In September (1850) the number of fishing vessels at the Southern Head amounted to one hundred or more . . . The presence of the Revenue Cutter alone prevented a scene of disorder and confusion, as well as great destruction of nets and other valuable property. After the nets were set for the night, all the fishing boats were ordered to return to the vessels to which they belonged; while the boats of the Cutter rowed guard during the night to prevent persons from injuring or stealing the nets. Yet, notwithstanding these precautions, and the exercise of great vigilance, nets were continually destroyed or stolen, especially during dark and windy nights, when the depredators could not be seen or heard. It was said, that boats with old scythes attached to their bottoms had been rowed swiftly among the nets, by which great damage had been done.[2]

Today, the Mananers are better protected from

poachers; and although they have to go farther afield for lobster and other fish, the abundance of their catch seems not to have diminished greatly in more than a century. "Everyone's working on the island," proud Mananers boast. This fact, of course is no small reason for the islanders' satisfaction.

Nevertheless, the men who fish such waters need to have much skill and endurance simply to survive, let alone bring in the enormous catches which they have obtained over the years. Accidents have happened, but fewer than one would suppose. They have usually involved strangers to the Grand Manan archipelago. In fact, when one middle-aged woman was asked if she did not worry about her husband when he was fishing, she replied at once in gently reproving tones: "Oh, no, not at all! He's been fishing these waters all his life. He knows what he's doing."

It has been said over the years that the island fishermen know the waters surrounding their island so well that even if a fog descends on the fishing grounds they can usually make home without much difficulty, being able to recognize each rock and ledge by the kind of rush or gurgle that the water around it emits. Their senses seem honed as precisely as an acute and sophisticated radar system. Consequently, it is hardly surprising that over the years, and particularly in the days of sailing ships, Grand Manan mariners were much in demand to work on vessels plying both American and Canadian waters — and above all, on ships entering the Bay of Fundy. No one, sailors reckoned, had a better understanding of the sea in its most upsetting moods than Grand Mananers, raised from infancy to interpret its most discordant music.

No one either has a stronger sense of the past and its shaping influences on the present than a Mananer. Nowhere else does one meet a whole population so up on its own history and so concerned with preserving it. The thriving museum and historical society attest to this, as well as the fact that almost any Mananer, even if not at all bookish, seems to be imbued with an encyclopedic knowledge of his island, past and present.

One of those responsible for the preservation of Grand Manan's heritage is L.W. Ingersoll, long-time editor of that most excellent and unusual journal, *The Grand Manan Historian*. The following excerpt from one of his many articles is indicative of his knowledge of his subject, his flair for narrative, and his recognition of the islanders' spirit of independence — his realization that they have always marched to a different drummer:

> Sheep were kept the year round on Kent, Outer Wood and some of the smaller islands of the archipelago, requiring two roundups, one in the Spring for shearing, and one later in the year for culling market lambs and mutton stock. Cattle, mostly young steers to fatten for winter beef, were pastured in the same places for about six months, requiring a roundup in the Fall.
>
> Young boys were hired for a few pennies a day to help with the roundups, usually just a case of driving docile animals into a corral. Often, however, as happened when the writer was involved on two or three occasions as a young lad, a mavarick [sic] would break away and elude its pursuers. Someone had liberated domestic rabbits on Outer Wood Island and these had multiplied ten thousand fold...Chasing a half wild steer over the crags and through the raspberry bushes with herring gulls screaming overhead in the fog, rabbits flushed and running for cover, with the risk of tripping in a burrow of a rabbit warren, or that of a Mother Carey's Chicken (Leach's petrel) — hooting and yelling to scare the steer in the right direction, was all heady stuff hardly matched by today's western classics on television.
>
> More than that, it must not be forgotten that this whole process of natural husbandry of sheep and cattle added an additional dimension to the security and benefits of life in this part of the world, too often derided by the well-meaning but grossly uninformed 'experts' on urban advantages.[3]

Although scores of knowledgeable and enthusiastic writers in *The Grand Manan Historian* have documented island life over the years, a flair for oral narrative is also very evident among islanders in general. For instance, on crossing to the mainland, particularly out of season, one is very likely to hear an islander instructing his visiting relatives on the history and geography of his island as the boat passes various landmarks — Whale Cove, Ashburton Head and others. On nearing Ashburton Head he will describe as vividly as if he had been there, the wrecking of the *Lord Ashburton* during the night of January 18, 1857, on the rocky promontory on the north end of the island which now bears the name of that ill-fated barque. The islander is bound to emphasize the fate of one of the eight survivors, a Danish seaman called James Lawson who scaled the cliffs and made his way to a barn where he was found the following morning still alive, though suffering severe frostbite. After being nursed for several days by the island people, Lawson was transferred to the marine hospital in Saint John where he remained for more than five years. Yet most of this time his thoughts must have kept reverting to the people of Grand Manan who had saved his life, because, as soon as he could move about he decided to return to the island and spend the rest of his life among its inhabitants. Despite the fact that he was permanently crippled after the shipwreck, with both feet partially amputated, he learned the trades of harnessmaker and shoemaker and practised these for the rest of his life on Grand Manan. He married an island girl and his descendents still live on the island.

Because such stories have been treasured and passed down from one generation to another, nearly every Mananer can trace his roots and those of his neighbors, knowing that they are all firmly anchored in the soil and rock of his island. Each individual who has been blown by chance or destiny into this archipelago, who took root and thrived here, seems to have found his own particular and accepted niche over the years.

These islanders have always looked out for each other. This is of course a basic survival rule of any remote society. Still it is interesting to note that, despite all the intrusions of the twentieth century, even now Mananers stick together. This is apparent everywhere, but perhaps nowhere more amusingly so than on the bulletin board on the ferry, where islanders are advised that the Island View Motel in Saint John offers Mananers $2.00 off the regular price of accommodations!

Such extended loyalties exist only in a very stable population, and the population of Grand Manan (about 2,600) has altered little in numbers, in background or in occupation in the last hundred years. In each generation some of the young people go away to make their lives elsewhere and enough remain to carry on. The school population remains constant at a little over five hundred.

Despite the Grand Mananers' strong feeling for the past, they have rarely been reluctant to accept contemporary innovations which they hoped would benefit their community. They have always been surprisingly up-to-date in the services and devices which they have imported. At no time was this more evident than in the 1880's.

For instance, during this time when so many communities had no newspaper at all, Grand Manan had two. Both editors were exceptional and controversial figures — declared rivals as well. Dr. G.N. Noyes ran *The Island Press* and J.B. Lorimer *The Island News*. Lorimer had already made a name for himself as a mainland journalist and author of a still fascinating and informative book, *History of the Islands and Islets in the Bay of Fundy* (1876).

Also early in the '80's — specifically in 1881 — Grand Manan established its own telegraph office. The islanders installed this service only seven years after the first successful cable across the Atlantic had been laid. Amusingly, as old records testify, Mananers at first used the telegraph system more frequently to get in touch with neighbors and family *on* the island than for making contact with the outside world. For instance, with the new equipment, family members who had gone visiting in the neighboring village could be checked on and called home if needed, and the doctor could at last be reached quickly and easily. Dr. J. F. MacCaulay's 'card,' issued early in this century, announced: "Calls answered any time of Day or Night to any part of Grand Manan. Can be called by telegraph up to 9 p.m."

Another step forward for Mananers in the 1880's was a regular ferry service. Subsidized by both federal and provincial governments, the first ferry went into service on July 1, 1884. Since just prior to this, lighthouses and fog alarms had been established at such treacherous places as Gannet Rock, Machias Seal Island, Long's Eddy and the Swallow Tail, the time seemed right for a ferry service.

All these developments paved the way for Grand Manan's acquisition of a telephone system in the following decade, only sixteen years after Bell had patented the device. By this time Mananers felt justified in claiming that they were just as up to date as people anywhere, yet not plagued by the usual unpleasant consequences of progress.

This is essentially true even today, for despite the islanders' ready acceptance of modern innovations, Grand Manan has not yet been spoiled by pollution — the price which so many other once beautiful places have had to pay for modernization and affluence. Although now threatened, it is true, by future radiation leaks from Point Lepreau nuclear reactor and oil spills from passing tankers, this island has so far been spared such horrors. Grand Manan, and indeed the whole surrounding archipelago, is still recognized as the special habitat and sanctuary of many species of marine and bird life, as well as one of the world's great beauty spots. Whales and dolphins cavort offshore — often accompanying the ferry on parts of its run; and birds nest by the hundreds of thousands on the outer, and now uninhabited islands.[4] Just as Audubon came to Whitehead Island in 1833 to observe and draw the herring gull, so contemporary scientists and wildlife enthusiasts flock annually to Machias Seal Island and other rewarding parts of this fertile domain to make their observations.

Squalid makeshift dwellings rarely mar the Grand Manan landscape. On the eastern and inhabited side of the island, sturdy, well-kept houses stand in green fields overlooking the sea. These fields, which once provided pasture for the islanders' livestock and food for their tables, are mostly untended now. The men are too busy fishing to bother with farming. The abandoned pastures and fields are nevertheless not without their charm. Here, within sight of the sea, one may ramble through June meadows where on low ground irises flame blue amid marsh grasses and on the uplands, strawberry blossoms gleam white against the dark earth, bright and numberless as stars in the milky way. Overhead, gulls shriek their delight in the clear salt air, and on the bay below sea ducks bob and murmur complacently among mats of seaweed and moored dories.

Behind the meadows, the woods, now mostly evergreen, begin. These woods stretch almost uninterrupted some four or five miles, depending on the island's varying width, to the formidable and uninhabited western cliffs. It was in these forests, and often several miles from the sea, that Mananers of old built hundreds of boats of all sizes. Oaks and pines did not, understandably, survive this industry — nor did boat building, like farming, survive the successful expansion of the island's fisheries.

But under the western cliffs another ancient occupation, dulse gathering, is still in full swing. In fact, now that dulse has been more widely recognized as a "health food," a sought-after commodity in specialty shops across the land, the dulse pickers are doing better than ever. Their favorite place is beneath the cliffs near Dark Harbour. No wonder dulse is purported to be imbued with mysterious properties, coming as it does from such a strange and enchanting place!

Dark Harbour is a place to catch the imagination of even the most prosaic individual. For instance, in the mid nineteenth century even Mr. Perley, a government employee sent to look into the harbour's commercial potential, fell under the spell of this natural wonder. His report is not the usual sort of tedious government document:

> Once within the sea-wall vessels are as completely land-locked, and may ride in as perfect safety, as if in an inland lake, however violently the tempest may rage without; and upon such a precipitous and iron bound shore as the western side of Grand Manan, with nothing but certain destruction to the tempest-tossed mariner who may be cast upon it, this sole place of safety should by all means, and under every consideration of humanity, be rendered easily accessible at all seasons, either by day or by night, and readily found. A few hundred pounds might well be spent in giving perfect access to this most singular and exceedingly safe harbour, accumulated by the mighty waves of many centuries. The largest ships may lie afloat within a stone's cast of the shore, riding safely with the smallest hawser, while a fearful surf thunders

upon the beach without, apparently with sufficient roar, and uncontrolled violence, to shake the island to its lowermost foundation.[5]

Because Mananers live in such an awesome natural environment, it is little wonder that they have always been deeply religious. A power beyond the understanding of man seems clearly to have been at work here. Yet religious life in the first century of settlement of Grand Manan flowed no more smoothly than the water around the island, and, paradoxically, occasioned the islanders considerably more discomfort than did the sea, which they had learned to cope with so readily.

At first they managed well enough with itinerant ministers from the mainland who seemed by and large enthusiastic about their mission to the island and sympathetic to its inhabitants. On Sundays when no qualified preacher turned up, the island schoolmaster read a service. However, increasingly the Mananers yearned for their own church and resident minister. Surprisingly, this yearning produced trouble.

Since the founders of the then new province had determined that New Brunswick should follow the British pattern of life as closely as possible, adherence to the Church of England was taken for granted. Money was given for the building of churches and support of clergymen of this denomination only. Mananers, like other New Brunswickers, were influenced by this fact. Thus, early in the nineteenth century the Church of England acquired over twelve hundred acres of woodland on Grand Manan; and the islanders, after raising most of the money for the construction of the church, proceeded to build it with their own hands — once again demonstrating their ability, determination and self reliance. By December, 1823, the island's first church, Saint Paul's, was ready for its first clergyman.

This cleric, a Mr. Griffin, turned out to be a disastrous choice. He was a quarrelsome Englishman with little love for his fellow man generally, and even less for Canadians — particularly those unfortunate and inept enough, from his point of view, to have gotten themselves stranded on such a God-forsaken rock as Grand Manan!

Mr. Griffin arrived on the island with his sisters in the spring of 1824 and for the next four or five years the islanders put up with his nagging, his bad temper, and his lack of understanding or sympathy for their lives and environment. That the islanders' religious zeal survived this man's ministry is in itself something of a miracle!

Eventually Mr. Griffin was succeeded by the Reverend John Dunn, a newly-ordained clergyman from Saint Andrews who, with his wife and child took up residence on the island in 1832. Mr. Dunn was, fortunately, not at all like his predecessor. He was hard-working, uncomplaining and faithful. We are told that "in matters spiritual Mr. Dunn achieved remarkable success."

But Mr. Dunn's success apparently infuriated the most influential man on the island, Mr. Wilfred Fisher, the magistrate and landowner who had been nicknamed "the Emperor of Grand Manan." Blinded by jealousy of Mr. Dunn, whom he saw as his rival in wielding power over the islanders, Mr. Fisher took steps to rid the island of the interloper.

Thus on October 9, 1838, an event occurred which unsettled the community for years afterward. On this night the church was burned — and in a tree near it was placed an effigy of Mr. Dunn dressed in "a long black waistcoat, satin vest, a pair of black pantaloons, white gloves and black boots. Arms and legs pinioned by cords to its side, the figure was swinging by the neck . . ."[6] Everyone recognized the clothes on the effigy as belonging to Mr. Fisher, and so it was on Mr. Fisher and two of his servants that suspicion for the crime fell.

In due course the three men were tried for their lives in the Supreme Court in Saint Andrews. Despite the fact that their guilt seemed obvious, they were exonerated, much to the disgust of the majority of the islanders. Mr. Fisher even returned to Grand Manan to assume all his former honors, including his duties as magistrate!

As the excitement faded, the island population remained generally demoralized. A cynicism concerning the proper functioning of the law dominated island thinking. Understandably, the next few years have been regarded as the darkest period the island has ever known. Although some positive steps were taken, such as the rebuilding of Saint

Paul's, in stone this time, it was generally a time of dispondency and even lawlessness.

Eventually, in 1844, Mr. Fisher had his way: Mr. Dunn left the island. No one came to take his place, and the bishop seemed reluctant to make the fatiguing and sometimes dangerous crossing to confirm new church members. Interest in the established church flagged. Itinerant Baptist and Wesleyan preachers were more favorably received than before. Gradually the majority of the Grand Manan residents shifted their religious affiliations from Anglican to Baptist.

This shift was accelerated by the appearance of the Reverend A. Taylor on Grand Manan. Like an old testament prophet, he told of seeing the island in a vision and of being sent there by God:

> Instantly I seemed to be on the deck of a vessel going upon surroundings I had never seen before. "My God," said I, "What is this?" and the answer came immediately. "This is Grand Manan, go there, and you will gather a church of 130 members and see much good done."[7]

Mr. Taylor's vision and ardor proved irresistible. Many Mananers were persuaded that he had indeed been heaven-sent. His inspired and high-powered evangelism left its mark, since to this day most of the islanders adhere to the faith into which their ancestors were baptised.

Some Great Spirit must still hover protectively over THE ISLAND, causing it to prosper and, at the same time, to be spared most of the curses of prosperity. Grand Manan, despite two centuries of settlement, can still inspire in the twentieth century viewer much of the wonder and delight which the first people sighting this island must have felt. No wonder Mananers are so content with their island!

1. *The Perley Report on the Fisheries of Grand Manan (1850), The Grand Manan Historian,* No. X, The Grand Manan Historical Society, p. 16.

2. *Ibid.,* p. 20.

3. *The Grand Manan Historian*, No. XIX, p. 25.

4. Of about a dozen small islands in the Grand Manan archipelago only Whitehead Island is still inhabited, and it has a contemporary population of several hundred. Its population has continued to grow because it is on the way (from Grand Manan) to the best fishing grounds. Because of the increase in population, however, the herring gulls no longer nest here.

5. *The Grand Manan Historian*, No. X, p. 22.

6. *The Grand Manan Historian*, No. XXI, p. 26.

7. *The Grand Manan Historian*, No. XIX, p. 34.

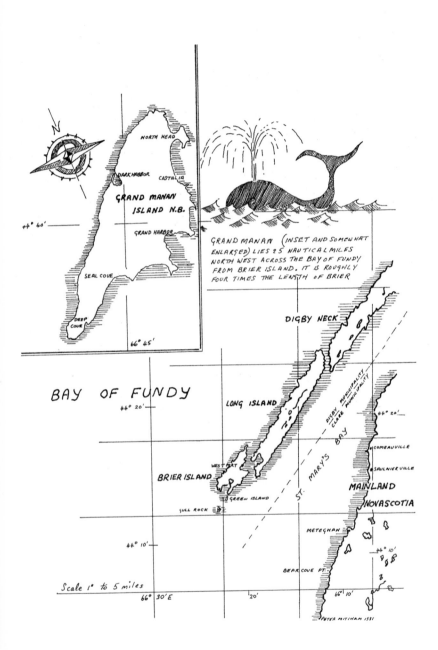

N

NORTH HEAD

DARK HARBOR   CASTALIA

GRAND MANAN
ISLAND N.B.

GRAND HARBOR

44° 40'

SEAL COVE

DEEP
COVE

66° 45'

GRAND MANAN (INSET AND SOMEWHAT
ENLARGED) LIES 25 NAUTICAL MILES
NORTH WEST ACROSS THE BAY OF FUNDY
FROM BRIER ISLAND. IT IS ROUGHLY
FOUR TIMES THE LENGTH OF BRIER

DIGBY NECK

BAY OF FUNDY

44° 20'

LONG ISLAND

DIGBY MUNICIPALITY
CLARE MUNICIPALITY

ST. MARY'S   BAY

44° 20'

COMEAUVILLE

SAULNIERVILLE

WEST PORT

BRIER ISLAND

GREEN ISLAND

MAINLAND
NOVA SCOTIA

GULL ROCK

METEGHAN

44° 10'

44° 10'

BEAR COVE PT.

Scale 1" to 5 miles

66° 30' E

'20'

66° 10'

PETER MITCHAM 1981

24

Chapter Two

BRIER ISLAND AND HER THOREAU OF THE SEA

It is known that a Brier Islander, fish or no fish on his hook, never flinches from a sea. He just tends to his lines and hauls of 'saws'. Nay, have I not seen my old friend Deacon W. C._____, a good man of the island, while listening to a sermon in the little church on the hill, reach out his hand over the door of his pew and 'jig' imaginary squid in the aisle, to the intense delight of the young people, who did not realize that to catch good fish one must have good bait, the thing most on the deacon's mind.

So writes Captain Joshua Slocum, the most famous Brier islander, in his internationally famous book, *Sailing Alone Around the World* (1900). These few lines not only indicate the qualities which distinguished Slocum and made him exceptional both as an adventurer and as a writer — but at the same time, point to the characteristics and state of mind which have distinguished the people of this island both before and after Slocum's time. A preoccupation with the sea, its moods and the creatures which inhabit it, an independent spirit, a quiet and unflinching courage and a droll, low-keyed sense of humor, expressed nearly always in metaphors plucked from the sea, are typical of both Slocum and his fellow Brier Islanders.

Small wonder the sea dominates the thinking of Brier Islanders! Brier is surrounded by some of the most treacherous stretches of sea in the world. The number of lighthouses on this island (three) — "a lighthouse a mile," according to one commentator — attests to the risks inherent in traversing these waters. Even Slocum, who in typical island fashion generally downplays the dangers of the sea, describes the "terrible thrashing" he got sailing over the southwest ledge off Brier "through the worst tide-race in the Bay of Fundy." Others have catalogued at length the foreign vessels wrecked off both Brier and Long Islands — as they have off Grand Manan. The winter of 1846, for instance, was reckoned to be especially bad for ships attempting to carry cargoes of lumber down the Bay of Fundy past Brier. Of twenty-five ships which started out, only nine were able to complete their trips.

Still, the local fishermen of Brier, like the Mananers, managed better. They learned early to cope with the worst the sea near their island could provide, and, as a reward for their stamina and vigilance were, again like their neighbors, the Mananers, provided with the most profitable living from one of the world's best fishing grounds. Fishing off Brier, too, was just the schooling that a mariner who was later to set the record as the first man to sail round the world single-handed needed. Slocum was to find, like other Fundy-trained seafarers, that neither Cape Horn nor the Barrier Reefs provide hazards any worse than those encountered daily near his boyhood home. Thus quite comically in *Sailing Alone Around the World*, Slocum wonders why he does not have more 'adventures' of the sort he sees and reads about. He does not, however, remark, as other writers have, that adventures tend to be the result of miscalculations.

With her tiller lashed, the *Spray* keeps to her course day after day whilst her captain at his leisure writes his log, consults the stars, observes the sea and its creatures, reads accounts of factual and fictional mishaps at sea from his well-stocked library, and from time to time, to left and right, witnesses the foundering of much more pretentious vessels than his own thirty-six foot sloop, a product by and large of his own "rough carpentry!" Like many of the men of Brier, Grand Manan, and so many other Maritime islands, Slocum's second trade — and second love — was boat building. And like his fellow islanders he was a great improvisor. To cut down a sail and make a new one, to shorten a boom (even while at sea), to replace a mast or a loose board, was the work of a few minutes — or at worst of a few hours. Nothing in this line daunted him.

Indeed, one of the most striking displays of his ingenuity occurred in 1887, almost ten years before he set sail on the *Spray*. Slocum, shipwrecked with his wife and his two youngest children on a South American beach, set to work with hand tools to make a boat to take them home — a distance of more than 5,000 miles. Out of the wreckage of the *Aquidneck* he made a new craft which he called the *Liberdale*, packed his family and possessions on board and sailed uneventfully home. The *Liberdale* was, by the way, some 35 feet long, close to the size of the *Spray* — 35 feet being, as Slocum himself said repeatedly, his lucky size for boats. No doubt his fondness for this size had much to do with his familiarity with this size of fishing boat during his childhood on Brier Island.

Brier Island is a typical Fundy isle, similar in many ways to her better-known sister island of Grand Manan — a mere twenty-five nautical miles distant. So striking are the similarities between these two Fundy islands, so subtle and only gradually and intermittently apparent their differences, that it is well worth one's while to stop for a moment and look at them side by side.

The rocky coastline and granite cliffs; the superb fishing; the huge colonies of sea birds and the ornithologists who come to observe them; the large, well-kept houses stretching along the eastern coast only; the obvious busyness and prosperity of the people, together with their friendliness; the early Loyalist settlement and continuing connection over the years with the United States — particularly with Maine, are all obvious points of comparison.

Then too the similarity in the shape of these two islands is uncanny. One can, of course, dismiss this immediately apparent resemblance by remarking that both have obviously been shaped by the same Fundy tides and currents. Yet none of the other Fundy islands has been cast in so similar a mold. The odd feeling of relationship between these two islands persists.

Brier was first settled a few years before Grand Manan when David Welch and his family arrived from Maine in 1769 and were soon joined by Robert Morrell. But the real influx of settlers to both islands took place about the same time — when the Loyalists arrived — on Brier in 1783 and on Grand Manan in 1784.

Brier is of course just a fraction of the size of Grand Manan, with a population in proportion. Four miles long, 1½ miles wide, and about 2,000 acres, Brier has a contemporary population of about 150; whereas Grand Manan is 15.6 miles long and 6.7 miles wide, 55 square miles in all, with a population of about 2,600. Although Grand Manan's population has remained stable for the last century, Brier has over the years experienced a dwindling population. Some authorities record a population high of 1,000 during one period in the nineteenth century. All seem agreed that there were at least as many as 800 residents. The statistics available for more recent years are quite precise: 1931 — 458; 1941 — 461; 1961 — 413; 1966 — 367. The difficulty in getting to and from the island is the reason cited for Brier's declining population. Yet when one compares the greater problems of travelling to and from Grand Manan, where no population slump has occurred, with the relative ease of getting to and from Brier, this reason seems insufficient.

Admittedly, getting to Brier takes considerable time and effort. There is the thirty mile drive down Digby Neck — not what it once was in the days of corduroy roads, but still arduous enough; the short ferry ride across Petit Passage; followed by a twelve mile drive down Long Island, and a final short ferry ride across Grand Passage to Brier. The descent on a steep and narrow ramp to the first ferry (linking Digby Neck with Long Island) is at low tide hair-raising to the uninitiated. No guard rail stands between the driver and surging currents which swirl right alongside the ramp. What if the brakes fail? All one's worst fears are exaggerated by the prominence of a government billboard just near the ramp disclaiming responsibility for accidents occuring here!

Still, after managing the first crossing, one quickly becomes almost as blasé as the 'natives' about the next, and is then in a reasonable position to assess and appreciate the positive aspects of ferry service in this part of the world. After all, a visitor soon feels ashamed of his fears when he learns that the high school students catch the ferry daily between Westport on Brier and Freeport on Long Island with as few forebodings as their mainland counterparts show when they board a bus.

The ferries to Brier (and Long) Island run all day every hour, and at night if necessary, cost only 50 cents return (the same price as when the first ferry began operations in 1822!) and are not overcrowded. One thinks by comparison of the two daily crossings (three in summer) to Grand Manan, the cost of $12 and up for a vehicle and driver, and the long waits which can occur. The Grand Manan ferry service is, by the way, a relatively recent innovation by Brier Island standards, having been on the run just under a hundred years — since July 1, 1884.

The comparison in this regard is hardly a fair one. Eighteen Fundy miles do not on Brier separate the traveller from the mainland as they do on Grand Manan. The two passages separating Brier and Long islands are hardly more than good-sized rivers — though indeed 'rivers' filled with treacherous currents. The dangers of these passages were in the early days of settlement of Brier considered to be so formidable that the original settlers had very little contact with mainland Nova Scotia. Their business dealings were with the New England States and the West Indies. Here again a parallel exists with the Mananers who, in the early days of settlement, were also closely allied with their American cousins. No wonder! After all, for the Mananers a crossing to the American side was a third of the distance to the Canadian side — no mean consideration when coping with Fundy fogs and tides.

Although the ferries are quick and reliable, the roads adequate, the visitor still cannot help wondering just how a Brier Islander would get medical aid in the event of an emergency or an accident. After all, the trip to Digby takes up to two hours by road and ferries, and there is no air service between Brier and the outside world as there is between Grand Manan and the mainland and between Pictou Island and the mainland.

Still, Brier Islanders are quick to dispel such fears and

doubts. "No problem at all!" one islander replied to a stranger's quip about being stranded helpless in emergencies at the end of the world. "The coast guard is always quick and ready to help. Why I lived for a while just outside Halifax and it took longer to get someone to hospital from there than it takes from Brier Island!"

Brier Island is certainly not a backward place. Brier Islanders, like Mananers, have never been slow to acquire modern devices which would improve the quality of their lives. They are isolated, but not cut off. For instance, both islands promptly acquired telephones shortly after their invention. By 1888 Brier Island inhabitants not only had telephones but had the head office of the telephone company located right on the island! Yet other islands of considerable size and importance in the Maritimes had to wait much longer for comparable services. Pictou Island, much to the chagrin of its people, had to wait until 1921!

Brier Island, in contrast to Grand Manan, has only one town, Westport. This village is stretched out along the eastern coast, facing the town of Freeport across Grand Passage on Long Island. As with Grand Manan's settlements which are also along its eastern shore, everyone in town has a view of the sea — and a most spectacular view it is! In the old days, before the big central wharves were built near the present fish plant, fishermen had their own wharves in front of their houses. Many of these still remain.

Westport is unique. Despite a similar hillside location on the eastern coast and comparable wealth (proportionate to population, that is), Westport does not have the same atmosphere as the villages on Grand Manan. In Westport the pace of life is slower, the visitors fewer. The main street along the water is narrow and paved, reminding one a little of how Cornish fishing villages must have looked before the tourists discovered them; for in Westport tourists are rare. Consequently, there are no tea shops, no inns or bed-and-breakfast boarding houses, no gift shops and no potters or painters attempting to introduce something of the charm of the surroundings into saleable works of art. Westport is charming, but it is strictly functional. It exists as it has always existed because of the needs of its people.

If the street along the water reminds the visitor of the old world, the houses on the hillside do not. They are distinctly Canadian — and Maritime. They are mostly large, sturdy, wooden frame houses, some of them of elegant design, painted in whatever colors suit the temperament of the owner — and the colors are of a considerable range. These houses have an air of stability, comfort and permanence. They appear to have been here for some time already, and look as if they will be a part of the scene for some time to come.

Inland the terrain differs from that of Grand Manan. Much of Brier tends to be boggy or swampy, and where trees grow they are less luxuriant than on Grand Manan. On the headlands, trees are replaced altogether by wiry grasses. There is even a considerable difference in this respect between Brier and Long Island where farming is still carried on and where trees flourish in many parts. On Brier even gardens are hard to find now — though early settlers apparently grew all their staples after enriching the soil with seaweed and fish. Today for a farmer or a lumberman, Brier is not the place to live. Its name of course indicates this. Brier apparently takes its name from the healthy crop of brambles and briers growing on the western and stormswept side of the island.

Like the briers, the people of this island are hardy and tenacious, survivors in a harsh environment. And if in their stubbornness the thorns are sometimes apparent, so are the roses. For the visitor, the flower on the brier is the kindness of the people. Their openness and good humor which are at once apparent to the newcomer to Brier, were clearly instrumental in shaping Slocum's own assessment of islanders world-wide, since he was later to make the generalization: "Islanders are always the kindest people in the world...."

That they are also the most independent is a fact which Slocum so memorably demonstrated. And while much of the world, through the international (though American-based) Slocum Society, continues to celebrate the remarkable accomplishment of the extraordinary Brier Islander who at fifty-one set out alone, without any money, in a homemade boat to sail around the world, and while both British and Americans still vie with one another to claim him as their own, the Brier Islanders have had little to say on the subject. After all, it's hard to impress a Brier Islander with independence and nautical prowess: It's just taken for granted that islanders know what they are doing at sea and trust their instincts in making decisions. If they feel called on to give an instance of the hardiness and determination of one of their own, instead of citing Slocum's achievement they are much more apt to recount how Christiania Davis, the widowed mother of nine children, walked the 386 miles to Halifax and back to sort out a squabble about the title to her land. The invincible Mrs. Davis returned of course with the deed and, not at all worn out by such an excursion, nor with raising her large family alone, carried on vigorously until she died on the island at the age of ninety-three (in 1889).

Still, if in the independent fashion of their kind, the people of Brier Island have their own heroes or no heroes at all, Slocum has become for much of the rest of the world a larger-than-life figure. Attempts to define and limit his accomplishments have always proved difficult. His essence is, to some extent elusive, rather like that of Antoine de Saint-Exupéry or Henry David Thoreau. And indeed Slocum has been called a "Thoreau of the sea." Both men were moved by the same sort of independent spirit; both were by and large ruled by an anti-materialistic outlook which enabled them to escape the fetters of conventional society; both loved nature and spent considerable time charting her moods; both built with their own hands their dwelling places — Thoreau his cabin, Slocum his boat; both decried conventional education as ineffectual and impractical, advocating actively doing rather than passively listening; both expressed themselves in homespun terms, using frequently metaphors harvested from their own understanding of earth and sea and human nature; both did all they could to avoid and destroy cant and hypocrisy — to find freedom close to natural sources. In this search for the free and the natural, they both criticized civilized man's propensity for confining himself and for ruining lives of happier and less sophisticated 'native' people.

Thoreau says,

I confess that I am astonished at the power of endurance, to say nothing of the moral insensibility, of

33

my neighbors who confine themselves to shops and offices the whole day for weeks and months, ay, and years almost together.... ("Walking," *Excursions*).

And:

> We talk of civilizing the Indian, but that is not the name for his improvement. By the independence and aloofness of his dim forest life he preserves his intercourse with his native gods, and is admitted from time to time to a rare and peculiar society with Nature.... Steel and blankets are strong temptations; but the Indian does well to continue Indian. (*A Week on the Concord and Merrimack Rivers*.)

Similarly Slocum contrasts the free and easy life of the South Sea islander with that of the civilized white man. He begins by quoting a Samoan chief:

> 'Dollar, dollar,' said he; 'white man know only dollar. ...Never mind dollar. ...Let us drink and rejoice. Let the day go by; why should we mourn over that? There are millions of days coming. The breadfruit is yellow in the sun, and from the clothtree is Taloa's gown. Our house, which is good, cost but the labor of building it, and there is no lock on the door....' (*Sailing Alone Around the World*).

If one is not exactly clear how Thoreau came by all his individualistic properties, other than by being influenced by his important friend, Emerson, and the stubborn Yankee independent spirit he was born with, one can argue that Slocum was in large measure shaped by the rigors of a childhood spent on Brier Island and by the vigor and independence of the people who were his neighbors there.

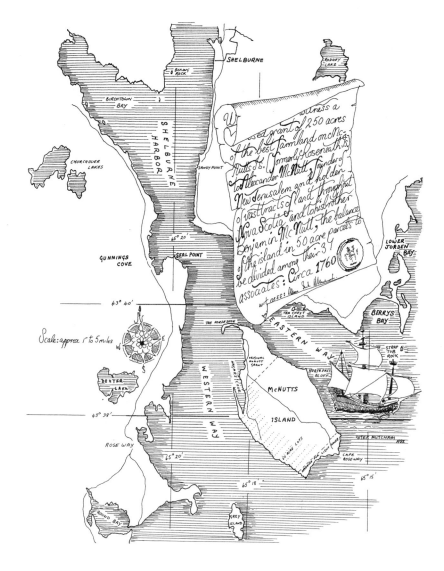

SHELBURNE

BOXINS ROCK

RIDLEY LAKE

BIRCHTOWN BAY

CHURCHOVER LAKES

SHELBURNE HARBOR

SANDY POINT

65° 20'

GUNNINGS COVE

SEAL POINT

LOWER JORDEN BAY

43° 40'

Scale: approx 1" to 5 miles

THE HORSE SHOE

TEA CHEST ISLAND

EASTERN WAY

BERRYS BAY

STRAP TUB ROCK

DEXTER LAKE

WESTERN WAY

ARISINAL McNUTT GRANT

NORTH EAST BLUFF

McNUTTS ISLAND

43° 38'

"PETER MITCHAM 1832

20 ACRE LOTS

CAPE ROSEWAY

ROSE WAY

65° 20'

65° 18'

65° 15'

ROUND BAY

KREY ISLAND

In witness a ___ sed grant of 250 acres of the best farmland on Mc-Nutts Is., formerly Roseneath Is, to Alexander McNutt, founder of New Jerusalem and holder of vast tracts of land throughout Nova Scotia and to his brother Benjamin McNutt, the balance of the island in 50 acre parcels to be divided among their 34 associates: Circa 1760

WITNESS: Alexander McNutt

35

Chapter Three

MCNUTT AND HIS ISLAND

No Maritime resident has had a more colourful career than 'Colonel' Alexander McNutt, and no small Atlantic island a more chequered history than the one which he called home and which now bears his name. McNutt, unabashedly self-promoted from Captain to Colonel, together with his shadowy 'associates' managed to gain possession of vast tracts of the Maritimes during the reign of George II and George III. One after another in an amazingly short time huge acreages near Truro, much of Pictou, Digby and Shelburne counties came under McNutt's jurisdiction. The powers-that- be, apparently under the spell of his enchanting Irish tongue, quickly fell for his schemes and dreams for Maritime development and settlement.

Even a detractor as powerful as Lieutenant Governor Jonathan Belcher was not influential enough to wreck McNutt's schemes or put an end to his land acquisitions. Still Belcher, though himself not a model of even-temper and rational judgement, seems not to have been too far out when in 1761 he assessed McNutt as "an erratic individual lacking in mental ballast, and one whose proposals needed to be watched."

Of all McNutt's proposals, the one which seemingly most closely touched his own heart and awakened his romantic imagination concerned the founding and settlement of an ideal community on what many considered to be Nova Scotia's finest harbour, and his own removal to the island at its mouth.

The utopian name he chose for the settlement, New Jerusalem, was later changed to the more utilitarian Port Roseway, and eventually to Shelburne; and the island, called Razoir[1] in Acadian times, and Roseneath by the famous cartographer DesBarres, became McNutt's Island. Surprisingly, this small island — 4 miles long, 2 miles wide at its broadest part, about 2,000 acres in all — is the only piece of land in all the Maritimes to bear the name of the man who once laid claim to such tremendous tracts.

Despite his dream for his New Jerusalem, it was on the island that McNutt himself chose to live. Like so many other early settlers throughout the Maritimes, McNutt clearly preferred island to mainland living, partly because of the security islands were thought to offer both human beings and their domestic animals, who, it was assumed, could roam safely without encountering such formidable predators as Indians, bears, and wolves. Such assumptions were often naive. The Indians, who had invariably been there first, often resented the white man's intrusion, and took steps to dislodge him.

Islands such as McNutt's were not, moreover, so easily tamed as their early inhabitants hoped. McNutt's has always defied the incursions of civilization. An island whose rocky soil and thick underbrush have withstood the plough and mower for centuries, it is still, as one Shelburne merchant remarked, "a very wild place."

The granite cliffs, the dense bush, and the fogs which so often wrap McNutt's in their cold, damp embrace did not deter McNutt. As was usual when he had a colonizing project in hand, he got together a group of 'associates.' On this occasion McNutt's associates numbered thirty-seven.[2] Each of these men received fifty-acre grants, many of which were practically inaccessible because of the rugged nature of the island and the general lack of landing places. As happened often with McNutt's land settlement ventures, few of the grantees ever took up residence and even fewer presisted with enterprises such as farming or fishing.

McNutt, with a shrewd eye to his own welfare, managed better. He and his brother Benjamin not only wangled 250 acres, but made sure that his acreage was the best piece of farmland. The McNutt's holding, moreover, conveniently gave on the only well-protected natural harbour on the island. The two brothers established themselves on this tract and did indeed take up farming, as is indicated on surviving tax assessment records. 'The Colonel,' acting true to form, managed to avoid most of the work. Leaving Benjamin to cope with the McNutt's Island property, he went off on excursions to the United States and elsewhere. In spite of this, he still seemed to regard the island as home, and it was to this spot that he returned periodically over the years. 'Colonel' McNutt seems to have moved to the American colonies about the time of the War of Independence. Eventually he died in Virginia. Benjamin is thought to have died crossing from the island to the mainland. As neither brother had children, the property, then in Benjamin's name, passed on to a Martin McNutt, cooper, "probably of Shelburne town."[3] He is thought to have been Benjamin's and Alexander's nephew.

Until recently Alexander McNutt has stood on record as the first to attempt to leave his mark upon this island; but it has been suggested that he was not the first. Several years ago strange, and then seemingly indecipherable, hieroglyphics were discovered on a rock near the present light station, where Barry Crowell, a light keeper, was burning brush. Photographs of the markings were sent to a recommended expert on such matters, Dr. Barry Fell, professor emeritus of Harvard University, who, after spending some years studying them, made pronouncements on their origin and meaning. Either the Carthaginians or their apparent protégés, the Micmacs, were, he stated, responsible for the odd message left on the rocks.

The message, translated, reads: "Inscribed and left behind as a memorial to (or by) Chief Kese." Perhaps the spirit of the Micmac Chief, Kese, uneasy for many centuries about being left behind by his followers, emerged from the fog at last to stir the romantic Celtic imagination of a susceptible McNutt, enticing him to live near the ghostly haunts of a then extinct culture.

The Micmacs (and perhaps the Carthaginians) were not the only people associated with this island before McNutt's time. The French had been there too. One of their settlements was just across from the island at the spot where Carleton

Village now stands, and the potential of the whole harbour region was as favourably assessed by the Acadians in and around 'Cap-Sable'[4] (Cape Sable Island) as it was by later settlers. Indeed, they even considered building a fort in this region (a project not realized, indeed, until 1942 when the Canadian government did in fact establish a fort on the island!) Not only did the French fail to build any fortifications in this bay, but no indications of their occupation of the island remain.

Whatever McNutt's aspirations on the island, he was not in the end much more successful than Chief Kese or the Acadians in leaving his mark. Except for his name on the map and a now almost overgrown clearing, farmed intermittently over two centuries by successful settlers, nothing remians to tell of McNutt's sojourn in this place.

Indeed no spot on earth seems to have withstood more remarkably man's attempts to etch his designs upon the land. Even the military occupiers of this island during the second World War did not greatly alter the face of McNutt's. The fortifications — gun emplacements and connecting tunnels — are now all but hidden by the heavy new growth of trees and underbrush. To find them one has to know where to look. And great is one's surprise on coming suddenly upon two huge cement craters, like two good-sized swimming pools, each with a massive gun in the centre, sunk in the middle of the forest. One gun now lies in pieces in its concrete pit; the other, intact, is aimed at the wall of spruces which has grown up between it and the sea. The technicians responsible for installing these guns must have taken their secrets to their graves, for later technicians failed in attempts to dismantle and remove these relics to the military museum to which they were assigned. So instead of hordes of tourists coming to marvel at their complex oddities, the deer, unimpressed, skirt these antique armaments in search of succulent new growth.

More useful and lasting legacies of the military are the sturdy wharf, protected by the encircling arm of the natural breakwater which extends from the edge of the original McNutt holding, and the gravel road which links this wharf to the lighthouse at the far end of the island. The wharf is now used by fishermen; the road by those who travel to the

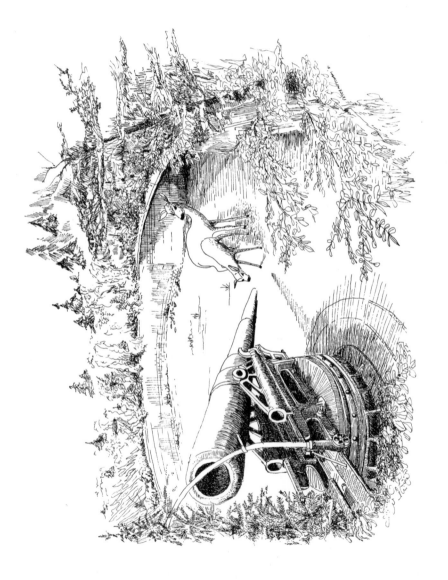

lighthouse or down the grassy trail which branches from it along Perry's Cove.

The gravel road to the lighthouse is not by mainland standards much of a road. Only wide enough to permit passage of one vehicle, alders and brambles seem intent on reducing even this narrow passageway. Each summer they engage in a silent struggle with the light keepers to close the gap, winning an inch or so each year.

There is a surprising tranquility on this road, a stillness, perfumed on warm summer days by berries ripening in the trapped sunlight and ferns pressed by passing deer or sheep. The only sounds are the calling and whirring of the many birds. Even the pounding of the sea does not penetrate to this road, and if one did not keep reminding oneself of the lighthouse destination and of the sea not far off to left and right, usually less than a mile away, one would imagine oneself some considerable distance inland.

Except for the keepers of the light, their families and one summer resident, the inhabitants who occupied the island as little as twenty-five years ago — strung out along Perry's Cove — have gone to the mainland where life, they concluded, would be less complicated. However, as one former resident who had lived on the island until she was sixteen recalled:

> Leaving the island didn't really simplify life as much as everyone expected. Certain things, such as shopping, were easier, I suppose. But other things — schools for instance — were more troublesome.
>
> At the time I didn't realize how well off I was at the island school. There were only six or seven of us for one teacher to cope with, so she was never harassed or bad-tempered. She always had lots of patience and time for each of us. It's really different with my children now on the mainland. I wish they could have the same chance, the same carefree childhood I had on the island. There, all my schooling was a positive experience. I really learned a lot — painlessly.
>
> It's funny, though, you never appreciate experiences like I had until they don't exist any more — because, at the time, I was as ready as anyone else to

come to the mainland. I just couldn't wait. It seemed so glamorous. I guess, above all, I wanted to have electricity which seemed, and I guess is, such a marvellous commodity.

Still, now when we go back to picnic on the island, I find it so special, ideal really, with the trees entwined over the road through the woods, (She is referring not to the lighthouse road, but to the grassy trail which branches from it along Perry's Cove.) and no sound except for the birds and the sea. It's protected there — warmer, as I remember it, and less windy than the mainland. I feel now that it's a perfect place to live — and yet there's no going back.

With one exception, the houses which this woman and her contemporaries occupied have long since burned or decayed beyond recognition. Today, only the first house along the Perry's Cove trail is still intact. This is because it was rescued just in time — some twenty years ago — by a woman who returns to McNutt's each summer. Apart from being painted and kept in repair, this place is much as it must have been when it was a year-round residence and post office as well. A glimpse of this simple and pretty dwelling resting by the sea in the summer sun causes the viewer to wonder about all the life which this small house has seen. The gnarled fruit trees surrounded by a long, low wall of stones, so laboriously piled years ago, attest to the industry and devotion of an earlier dweller — as well as to the difficulty of cultivating such rocky ground. One wonders what happened to him after he abandoned his island home.

The walker who carries on up the woodland track, now trodden habitually only by sheep, is saddened by the fall of the other old houses. It is now too late to rescue them. Human endeavor, a sense of community, no longer have any place here. Today, no one would ever guess that just over a century ago — on May 11, 1880 — a boat, the *Laconic* (tonnage — 15:35) was built and launched here for its owner, Samuel H. Perry, an island resident.

Even seventy years ago the community seemed busy and contented. There is, for instance, no indication in the columns relating weekly events of McNutt's Island in the

Shelburne Gazette and Coastguard for the two or three years preceding the outbreak of the first World War, that the people's way of life on the island was threatened. Frequent comings and goings, winter and summer, of the Snows, the Rapps, the Gouldens and other island families are recorded. The entries are all commonplace and down to earth, typical indeed of rural reports everywhere, even today.

For instance, here are two entries for December 1913: "Mrs. Martha Snow returned home (to Gunning Cove) after a pleasant visit with friends at McNutt's Island," and "Mr. George H. Rapp of McNutt's Island was successful in killing five ducks at one shot and wounding two or three more one day last week." The entry of October 30th of the same year reads: "A party of young folks from McNutt's Island called on friends here (Gunning Cove) on Sunday afternoon."

There seems no clue in such mundane commentaries to make the reader think of disillusionment or disaster or to prepare him for the flight of the inhabitants some few decades later and the subsequent neglect of their dwellings. Perhaps the desolation of these ruined houses has given rise to hints from nearby mainlanders that a certain undefined strangeness haunts the island now. One man told me:

> Snakes and toads, so big you wouldn't believe your eyes, live over there. I touched what I thought was a big stone with the toe of my boot. Well, it jumped and gave me a real surprise. It was only a toad — but what a toad! It was ten times the size of any normal toad I've seen around here. And the snakes! ...They're rare big black ones. I used to think I might like a place on the island sometime, a hunting camp at least, but I don't know...I feel sort of strange there. I could tell you other things you wouldn't believe....

Although several others repeated these stories, the wife of the present light keeper, twenty years resident on McNutt's, said that she had never seen any strange creatures on the island.

> I've spent hours and hours — longer than anyone else — right where the snakes are supposed to live, near those concrete bunkers the soldiers built, and I've never

seen one. This was when the children were little and I used to take them up there where it was protected, sunny and out of the wind. Day after day I was there and saw nothing.... Maybe the snakes didn't come out because they know I'm not frightened of them!

Whatever the facts in this particular instance, it is the light keepers and their families who have provided whatever sense of continuity has existed on McNutt's in the past two hundred years. They have been not only keepers of the light but guardians of the island as well. They have watched over it in all its moods. Frequently they have been, as they are today, the island's only permanent human residents.

The first Cape Roseway lighthouse on McNutt's Island, erected in 1788, was one of the earliest in the Maritimes. The third light station built in Nova Scotia — after Louisbourg (1737) and Sambro (1752) — it was, like them, constructed in the old world fashion. It was also, in the manner of those times, built to last — and last it did, until just over twenty years ago when it was destroyed by fire and replaced by a conventional modern structure.

The original McNutt's Island lighthouse must have resembled a fortress. Its foundation was of massive granite blocks cut from the rocky cliffs on which it was perched. The walls were six feet thick and the blocks held together with mussel shells burned and ground into mortar. The upper part of the lighthouse was wood and in the interior great beams of oak and hackmatack were visible. There was a thick reinforced iron door to prevent pirates breaking in. As if the Cape Roseway light station had been some arctic outpost, seal oil was the fuel which the first keeper, Alexander Cocken, used.

In the pattern followed by so many Maritime light keepers, Cocken and his son, also called Alexander, devoted nearly all their lives to their light station: the father from the time the first foundation stone was laid in 1787 until his death in 1812; the son, from the time of his father's death until his own retirement (and subsequent death) in 1861. Together they kept the light at Cape Roseway for seventy-three years — something of a record!

The monumental nature of their task and achievement, together with their own versatile and independent natures, becomes apparent through the letters, still extant, which they wrote to Joseph Howe and other members of the Nova Scotia provincial legislature over these years. These letters had to do chiefly with maintaining the light station and the three miles of road joining it to what Cocken described as the only possible landing place for fuel oil — a tiny cove on the north-west end of the island.

We see the father reluctantly (in the year of his death) ask the government for £30 or £40 to help maintain the road, to hire men and build it up in the swampy places. The task of keeping the road passable was, we hear, complicated by the fact that only two men on the island were "bound to perform Statute Labor."

The road, was, however, only one of the Cockens' problems. Both mention that, because of the island's location, they were forced to pay two or three times the mainland prices for all commodities. Also, surprising as it may seem to us, they had difficulty finding assistants who were sufficiently trustworthy and dedicated to the task of lightkeeping.

Once a suitable assistant was found, the new problem was paying him. As the £100 salary paid the light keeper was not enough for him to provide for an assistant, and as the government seemed reluctant to vote any additional funds, Cocken the younger took matters into his own hands and decided to earn the extra money which his assistant would cost him. He did this by setting up a school for boys and young men at the light station. He ran this school for 24 years (from 1836 to 1860), charging each scholar £20 for nine months of tuition together with room and board at the light station.

Despite his many responsibilities and inadequate remuneration, Cocken apparently found life on McNutt's satisfying. This is brought out in his letter of retirement. In this letter he asks for a replacement and recommends the situation to his successor:

> ...a considerable spot of land is under good tillage order, producing hay sufficient for at least 3 cattle and by cultivating some marsh adjoining additional wild hay might be cut — and any quantity of wild run for sheep; besides a good spot for a vegetable garden and

potato ground near the dwelling house. The situation, under such circumstances, would make it valuable to any respectable family whom the Government would select for this truly desirable employment.

Some of the residents of Shelburne County still remember hearing about Mr. Cocken's school. One of these, Mrs. Hagar, who now lives on Ragged Island, recalled that her grandfather had actually attended it. And doubtless due to this connection, her father eventually held the job as keeper of this light. "And now that's all you'll ever see of the old building," she remarked, pointing to a fragile glass ball on which a small white lighthouse is painted.

"No human being seems to have made much of a mark on that island — at least not for long," Mrs. Hagar continued. "It is not like other places. The woods and the sea almost seem anxious to be rid of the people, and the people seem to have no clear idea of continuity. Even the graves in the graveyard have no inscriptions, only fieldstone markers ... and I do not think I could find the old burying ground any more for the trees.... Could you?" she asked, turning to her brother. He shook his head.

The present light station with its freshly-painted buildings, near fences and closely-cropped grass is undoubtedly attractive. Unfortunately however, this station has been made to resemble as closely as possible other contemporary lighthouse compounds where the government has left its stereotyped imprint as surely as with a military installation.

However, the military effect is mitigated by the presence of sheep[5] roaming both inside and outside the fences and by the narcissus which have run wild and sprung up in widely separated clumps in the places they have chosen. Above all, it is absolutely dispelled by the warmheartedness and spontaneity of the chief light keeper and his family. They are living, irrefutable arguments against automation — automation which has already come to so many island lights, and will doubtless soon come to this one. One of these days there will be no coffee or chowder, no friendly concern or humorous anecdotes to cheer the cold, wet and weary voyager.

It is on this light station and on the accompanying foghorn which the fishermen, and indeed all who travel this stretch of coast by sea, depend. At night, in storm or fog, they beam and boom their warnings across the harbour and out to sea, telling all those who watch and listen that they must not venture near the granite rocks which line the sea face of McNutt's. Not every mariner has seen or heard the warnings, as the record of wrecks on these rocks indicates — but considering the danger and the great number of comings and goings here winter and summer, in fair weather and foul, for centuries, disasters have been few when one compares McNutt's with islands so notorious for marine disasters as Scatarie, Grand Manan, Cape Sable, Saint Paul's, Seal, and of course, Sable.

So although over the years men have come and gone from McNutt's — among them Kese, the Acadians, the Cockens, and McNutt too — the strategic importance of the island itself has not diminished. It is as important now as it has always been to seafarers entering or leaving the wonderful harbour which it guards: as important as it was to the first Loyalist settlers who were, it is claimed, guided to Shelburne, past the island by the first DeMings, resident in what is now Charleton Village; or to the military in the last war, who imagined that this was just the harbour the Germans would wish to control. A belief in the continuing significance of McNutt's Island is often reiterated by local fishermen who state matter-of-factly: "We all take our bearings from this island."

1. The island was called 'Razoir' up until 1755, the time of the expulsions of the Acadians, and the whole of what is now Shelburne Harbour was designated as 'Port-Razoir.' According to Clarence d'Entremont (*Histoire du Cap-Sable de l'an mil au traité de Paris*, Hébert Publications, Eunice, Louisiana, 1981, Vol. 3, p. 1156ff.), Port Roseway, as the English called the region after the expulsion, was simply a mispronunciation of the French name. M. d'Entremont says that there are several explanations,

neither totally convincing, for the name 'Razoir.' One is that a part of the harbour is in the shape of an old-fashioned razor; the other that it is named after the large number of razor clams found here. 'Roseneath,' DesBarres' name for the island, like so many of the other place names he used, did not stick.

2. M. d'Entremont, like so many other scholars, has referred to W.O. Raymond's article, "Colonel Alexander McNutt and the Pre-Loyalist Settlements of Nova Scotia" (Royal Society of Canada, 3rd Series, Vol. V, 1911, Sec. II, pp. 23-115), which states that McNutt had eighty-seven associates. This is clearly a mistake on Raymond's part since the original map clearly shows thirty-seven.

3. Genealogical records, Shelburne museum.

4. M. d'Entremont points out that Port-Razoir was at the eastern limits of the Acadian 'Cap-Sable' settlement.

5. The Sheep on McNutt's, as on a smaller island out from it — Grey Island — forage for themselves year-round. In the winter when grass and other vegetation on which they usually feed is no longer available, they survive on seaweed thrown up on the beach at high tide or exposed at low tide. Records show that early settlers on the islands in the Grand Manan archipelago also let their sheep fend for themselves all year in this way. Obviously such a practice has always been limited to the ice-free coasts of the southern horseshoe of Nova Scotia (from Shelburne around to Yarmouth) as well as to some of the Fundy islands.

50

Chapter Four

BIG TANCOOK AND EAST IRONBOUND ISLANDS: OF IRON MEN AND WOODEN BOATS OF CABBAGES AND KINGS

Tancook, seven miles out from Chester in Mahone Bay, faces the open sea. Ironbound, four miles beyond Tancook, receives the full force of Atlantic winds and waves. Both islands are rockbound, the home for more than two hundred years, of some of Atlantic Canada's most remarkable iron men and wooden boats. They are among the largest and are certainly the most famous of the estimated 365 islands[1] (one for every day of the year) in Mahone Bay. Tancook is known for its remarkable Tancook schooners and outsize cabbages; Ironbound as the setting of Frank Parker Day's novel, *Rockbound* (1928). But whereas Tancookers never seem tired of hearing eulogies about their prowess as builders of boats and makers of sauerkraut, Ironbounders clearly wish that the outside world had never heard of them through Day's book.[2]

Boats have been a priority for the people of all these islands for the last hundred years. Little wonder! Their lives depended on them. Over the years the most famous of these were probably the Tancook whalers, schooners built on the Tancooks which were generally reckoned to be the fastest and most seaworthy boats to be found. They have become legendary. Not only were they the most reliable of fishing schooners, but their owners, who were usually also their

51

builders and skippers, counted on being able to win a race against any yachtsman — and that, after a full day's fishing! It must be remembered too that the day's fishing for the men of these islands has always begun in the wee hours of the morning and continued until late afternoon — a fact attested to both by contemporary observation and by Day's book.

One old-timer's account of the Tancook whalers (or schooners) and the men who built and sailed them, throws considerable light on both men and craft:

> The Big Tancook whaler had a sharp (or Pinkey) stern and the rudder outdoors. Whalers were schooner-rigged and proved themselves wonderfully seaworthy and made a good name for themselves wherever they sailed. The first whaler was built at Southeast Cove, Big Tancook, by Alfred Langile about 1880.... All boats had brown tanned sails. You never saw a white sail those days on a fishing boat. They made this dye by boiling black spruce bark with more gum attached the better, in great iron pots holding from 50 to 100 gallons, adding rigging tar and some logwood bark according to your taste for color. They did this to preserve the sails and fill up the pores in the cloth, the better to hold the wind. Sails thus treated you had to wear out. They never got mildewed or rotted out.
>
> The whalers were schooner-rigged, mainsail, big foresail, jib and staysail. ...a word about the old timers' big foresail. It sheeted away back of the mainmast to the standing room, had a heavy hardwood club with iron strap where the sheets hooked. In tacking, one man caught that club under his arm and walked around mainmast and hooked sheet on other side. Woe betide you if you lost your hold on that club! If there was a good breeze you were liable to get your ribs or head cracked, but they sure were a driving sail. The staysail was another very important sail on those boats and I don't think there is any man in the world that could beat the Tancookers in making and getting the most out of staysails. (That is the fisherman type). A Tancooker always carried his staysail to windward of foresail, had

two sheets on it and when tacking he let his forehalyard go and let staysail go around forepeak quickly, hoist it to windward and sheet it home. In racing when running before wind, wing and wing, or as the Tancook fisherman called it, "Split Open", they had a pole to which they attached staysail and hoisted it to the topmast, making a squaresail out of it, which they called "scandalizing the staysail". Anyway it was very effective. I can still remember some of the old time greats that were renowned for their ability to handle a boat in any kind of weather — the Big Tancook David Baker "Old Shop" was, I believe, the daddy of them all, closely followed by Al Langile, Hip Baker, Zip Wilson, Wesley and Leander Young....

Ragattas started the first yacht racing.... Randolph Stevens and brothers were herring fishing in 'the Togo' (a boat built for them by Amos Stevens, their father). Hearing there was a fisherman's race in Halifax, and boats from Cape Sable and Canso were entered, so nothing must do but hustle home, throw out fish and gear and make off in the night. No time to stand boat ashore and clean bottom. Just made it in time to enter — and won the race.[3]

Although the Stevens, Youngs and others no longer build boats on the islands, the craft has not died out. David Stevens, for instance, still carries on the tradition of his Tancook forebearers in his boatyard on Second Peninsula, by water only a short run from the islands. Here, Tancook whalers, schooners differing from the originals chiefly in the elegance of their fittings, are still hand-crafted for particular and discerning yachtsmen. In the boatyard, craftsmen still sandpaper huge masts by hand — a rare sight in these days of assembly-line production.

Despite the fact that the Tancook Islands and Ironbound are now most frequently associated with boats and fishing, these were not the main concerns of the original settlers. The pioneers, chiefly of German origin, were farmers. They were drawn to the islands of Mahone Bay partly because these were considered good safe places to let stock run without having to worry at first about fencing. The land was, moreover, well-treed so that building material and firewood were immediately at hand. Records from 1788 concerning Tancook indicate that the island then had a climax forest of hardwoods. We are told specifically: "It is in general good hardwood land — beech, birch, and maple, and some oak, and ash.... Upon a moderate calculation, there may be about ten thousand cords of wood, and some timber trees for building." The settlers soon discovered that, once cleared and fertilized with seaweed and fish, their island land would produce abundant crops of hay and vegetables. In 1829 Haliburton remarked that the families of 'The Great Tancook' "derive their subsistence wholly from tilling the land."

'The Great Tancook' was, by the way, not always so named. Back in 1760 when the island was first settled, the famous explorer-cartographer, Joseph Frederick Wallet DesBarres,[4] christened the island 'Royal George' in honor of his king and patron, George III. However, like so many place names — including Mecklenburg Bay (now Mahone Bay) — which Desbarres initiated, 'Royal George' did not stick. Islanders abandoned the royal name for the indigenous Indian name, 'Tancook', which means "facing the open sea". And so, facing outward to Ironbound and to the Atlantic beyond it, the independent and self-sufficient inhabitants seem from the earlier days to have thought little of the powers across the sea. They ruled their own island kingdom wisely, without pomp and ceremony, attending to the cultivation of its productive soil.

The most successful and prolific crop on Tancook has always been cabbage — cabbage to ship abroad and cabbage for the islanders' favorite German dish, sauerkraut. For generations now these islands have been famous for the size and quality of the cabbages which they have produced in abundance. In the nineteenth century, schooner loads of cabbages were shipped to Europe where, apparently, they were much valued for their superior quality. Judge DesBrisay who was something of a horticulturist and island traveller in his day, has recorded in his *History of the County of Lunenburg* (1895) the size of several of these cabbages: "In November, 1894, Mr. Sylvester Baker of the Island (Big Tancook) pulled two (cabbages) from his field, one of which weighted 25 1/2 pounds and the another 23 1/2 pounds."[5]

An addiction to sauerkraut is apparently no longer confined to the islands, or indeed to Lunenburg County. Sauerkraut has become a favorite dish for much of the population of Nova Scotia's South Shore. One former Tancook islander, now a mainland resident, described how he had grown cabbages and made sauerkraut all his life, and how, even since his retirement, although he has given up growing cabbages, he has still continued to make sauerkraut. "I can never make enough of it," he remarked. "I just could never guess how much sauerkraut the people of this shore get through in a year. You'd think sometimes they ate nothing else!"

Fields of cabbages are still to be seen on Tancook and Ironbound, and on Tancook particularly the visitor is very much aware of the numerous and meticulously-tended kitchen gardens. This makes Tancook an exception to the rule which seems to hold for most other Maritime islands where fishing is big business: that the better the fishing, the fewer the gardens.

Although Big Tancook Island and Ironbound are clearly sister islands, a contemporary visitor is at once more aware of their differences than of their similarities. While he may observe that both islands are similar in shape, that both were settled in a comparable way — with settlement and cleared land in the middle and the woods (now chiefly spruces) at either end, that the founding people were of the same stock (closely related indeed), that both islands depend on fishing and are prosperous — it is nevertheless immediately apparent that Ironbound appears to have altered little in more than half a century, whereas Tancook clearly belongs in the late twentieth century. The description of Ironbound in Day's book could have been written yesterday:

> The island, elliptical in shape, was but a mile long and perhaps a half mile wide in its widest part, and consisted of two rounded spruce-clad knolls, at eastern and western ends, with a cleft between them. In the northern end of this cleft or shallow valley stood the fish houses and dwellings.... Throughout the valley from sea to sea, were fields of rank timothy and rich garden plots

for growing potatoes and cabbages. Two of the hills on the western end had been cleared and turned into hay-fields....In rough weather, when winter seas broke on the southern bar, spray and blown spume flew clear across the valley to the northern shore.[6]

Even today, the ways of doing things are still the same: "As the seas often run fiercely even on the northern and sheltered side of the island (where one lands) Rockbound (Ironbound) boats never lie at a mooring but are hauled out high and dry as soon as they touch the launch."[7]

There are a number of reasons for the differences in the two islands. One of these is evident as soon as one steps off the boat. Vehicles are rarely visible on Ironbound; on Tancook they are everywhere. Aesthetically this is important. The visitor to Ironbound who walks along the narrow track which the island's one tractor and truck have made, feels a great tranquility. Here is peace. Not only has he escaped from the hectic pace set elsewhere by the automobile, but he has also come far from the eyesores of contemporary civilization produced by piles of rusting metal dumped in fields and woods. On Ironbound only cranberries lodge in the clearings between the spruces; on Tancook a huge pile of rusting metal not far above the wharf attests to the dominance of the automobile and its attendant problems here.

Of course, there are reasons for the differences. Tancook is more than twice as big as Ironbound, with a very much greater population. Tancook is roughly three miles long and one mile wide, whereas Ironbound is about a mile long and half a mile wide at its widest part. Tancook has some 150 residents and quite a number of summer visitors; Ironbound has 12 families which are extensions of two — the Youngs and the Fincks — and few visitors. Because of the size of Tancook and its considerable population, vehicles — and large numbers of them — are almost inevitable. And moreover, because Tancook has been shared out among so many individuals, inevitably it cannot be cared for in the way that Ironbound's two extended families care for it.

Paradoxically Tancook's very accessibility — by the ferry's daily runs to Chester, summer and winter — has made life not only easier, but also somewhat less individual than it once was. Since islanders no longer risk their lives pushing through rough seas or across half-frozen ice to get the doctor,[8] and since it is no longer necessary to depend for long stretches at a time on what the island can produce, Tancook has tended to become more like everywhere else. Indeed, the ferry service to Chester is now so dependable and regular that the children, after completing grades primary to six on the island, commute daily to and from Chester to school. For them the ferry is no different than a school bus is for their rural mainland contemporaries. On Ironbound, since commuting is out of the question, a tiny school is maintained for students up to, and including grade ten.

Travel by boat to Tancook Island from Chester is simplified by the protected nature of Mahone Bay, and of course by the fact that the Bay is not, in our time, sufficiently ice-bound during the winter to interfere with the runs of a large and sturdy vessel. Things were once very different here, however — and not too long ago. Such an elaborate ferry service is a relatively new convenience for the islanders, who first started agitating for a government-run or subsidized ferry boat in 1934. The first ferry was the *Gerald L.C.*, a fishing schooner converted into a deck boat. It was replaced in 1942 by the *S. Mason*, a motor boat, and in 1945 by the *T.I. Service*, which was specifically designed as a ferry boat and was built at Mason's shipyard on Tancook Island. Once the *Shoreham* took over this run it was clear that a modern era of island travel had begun.

Before the inauguration of a dependable ferry service, travel between island and mainland was often a precarious venture, particularly in winter. Difficulties were compounded by the fact that winters in the early part of this century, and throughout the nineteenth, seem to have been more severe than they have been of recent years. For instance, Judge DesBrisay states that during the winter of 1821 Mahone Bay was frozen from Chester to Tancook "and loaded teams passed between the two places." We are told that during much of that winter vessels had to anchor at Green Island (some 16 miles from Chester and about 9 from Tancook). 1821 was apparently not such an exceptional year in the nineteenth century. Again in 1845 and in 1875 the bay was ice-bound — and until April!

Even in the early years of this century the Bay was, according to records, often partially frozen some distance out from the shore, so that boats sometimes came to the edge of the coastal ice from the island to pick up or let off passengers. Such dangerous travel was necessitated particularly when the doctor was needed on the island. The old-fashioned doctors, like Dr. Zwicker of Chester, took such trips as a matter of course in open boats, often in the dead of night and during storms.

In summer, however, the direct route between Tancook Island and Chester has always been travelled with much ease, even in a small boat which need never be far from land and from the protection it offers from the sweep of the wind. Everywhere islands, many of them resembling oversized sea urchins, are visible. According to authorities as seemingly remote from one another as DesBarres (*Atlantic Neptune* — 1763-75) and Clarke, Penner and Rogers (*Cruising Nova Scotia* — 1979), navigation in summer has always tended to be easy within this bay for the reason just mentioned and because the channels are for the most part deep and clear.

Still, the Tancookers and Ironbounders have little time to linger in the lee of tranquil and picturesque islands, waiting for winds to rise or fall. Whatever the weather, they are mostly outward bound. Long before the pleasure craft began to crisscross the sheltered reaches of the bay, the islanders in their brave and brightly-colored fishing boats have turned their backs to the Bay and have headed out to the fishing grounds.

1. Only one other group of Nova Scotia's island clusters is reckoned to be so large — the Tuskets. According to Clarence d'Entremont's *Histoire du Cap-Sable*, this group too is thought to have about 365 islands.

2. This has partly to do with the way Uriah Yung, nicknamed 'the king of Rockbound,' is depicted. Grasping and greedy, unwilling to recognize the rights of others, he emerges from the pages of the book as an autocratic ruler, similar in many ways to Mr. Fisher, 'the emperor of Grand Manan.'

3. "Reminiscences of an Old Timer — Edmund Fader (1959)," *History of Chester*, Women's Institute, 1967.

4. DesBarres' map shows a handful of habitations just near the island's contemporary wharf.

5. DesBrisay, *History of the County of Lunenburg*, p. 458.

6. Day, *Rockbound*, p. 69.

7. *Ibid.*, p. 23.

8. A situation described in *Rockbound*.

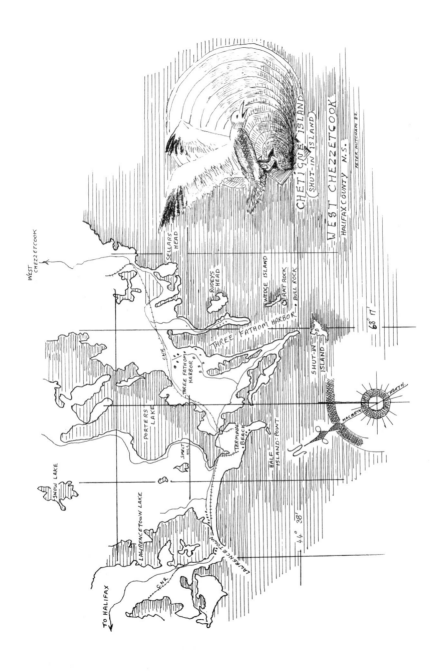

CHETIGNECT ISLAND
(SHUT-IN ISLAND)

WEST CHEZZETCOOK
HALIFAX COUNTY N.S.

PETER PHITCHAM 81.

WEST CHEZZETCOOK

SELLARS HEAD

RUDEYS HEAD

WEDGE ISLAND

FLAT ROCK

BULL ROCK

THREE FATHOM HARBOR

C.N.R.

THREE FATHOM
HARBOR
P.O.

P.B.

SHUT-IN
ISLAND

63° 17'

PORTERS LAKE

SMELT HILL

CLEARWATER BEACH

HALF ISLAND POINT

MAC BETH

NORTH

SNOW LAKE

LAWRENCETOWN LAKE

LAWRENCETOWN

C.N.R.

44° 38'

TO HALIFAX

61

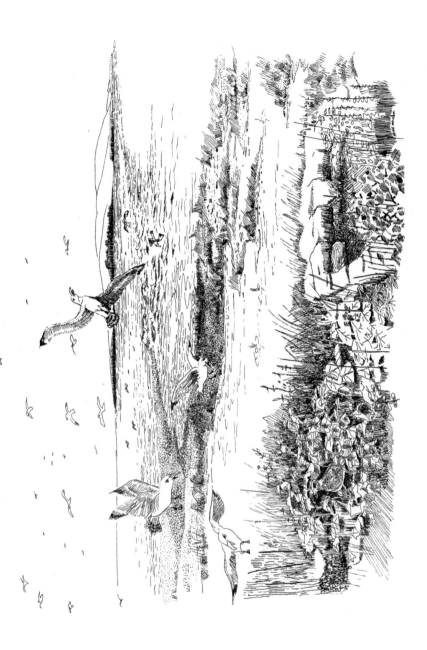

Chapter Five

THE MYSTERIES OF CHETIGNE —
OR SHUT-IN-ISLAND

"There is a lot of fact mixed with the fiction. I moved to Three Fathom Harbour in 1920 and we lived at the end of the Three Fathom Harbour Head. Chetigne Island is right off the head and is connected to the mainland by a reef. The reef could be seen from our place when the water was really calm. It was very hard to see from a boat though, and there were a couple of ships wrecked on that reef. Years ago, before my time, one could walk out to the island via the reef, but it has been washed away over the years. I have been out to the island and seen the remains of an old building. Lots of people will tell you about the light they have seen on that island. We always said it was a ghost."

— Mrs. Levina LeBlanc
Chezzetcook

"Mrs. Kate Misener recalls a story often told around Chezzetcook of a man who lived and died on an island in this area. Legend has it that he ws a Frenchman of noble birth, and that he sought refuge on the island to escape imprisonment for a crime."

— Chezzetcook Historical Society

With Chetigne — or Shut-In — Island the strands of fact and fiction are indeed so closely woven that the keenest eye finds them difficult to separate. Even the name is something of a puzzle. Shut-In is the name which has appeared on maps since at least 1818,[1] yet Mrs. LeBlanc, the former resident of the headland closest to the island, referred to it quite spontaneously as 'Chetigne.' Moreover, about the same time that Mrs. LeBlanc lived on this headland, Margaret McLaren, an inhabitant of the nearby town of Chezzetcook, wrote a novel describing the physical aspects of the island virtually as it appears today, except that the stone house of her story is now in ruins. She called her book *Chetigne Island* (1916).

The island, a small, flat, treeless[2] sliver of land just outside Three Fathom Harbour, is easy to locate. From the fishermen's wharf it seems little more than a stone's throw off Three Fathom Harbour Head. Yet, despite this, fishermen are reluctant to take their boats out to this island unless the tides are just right.

If, for instance, a visitor asks about going out to Chetigne in the spring, almost any of the local fishermen will insist adamantly, "Now's no good time to land on Chetin'. Better wait a couple of months... The nip's[3] too high to get on there now."

'Shut-In' seems to be, as some have speculated, a corruption of the French name 'Chetigne' — the change having taken place close to two hundred years ago when Anglophones, branching out from Halifax into the then predominantly Acadian region of Chezzetcook presumably thought that Chetigne sounded like 'Shut-In.' It is the same sort of linguistic aberration which occurred in Shelburne County when the French 'Razoir' became the English 'Roseway.' Today both the French and English fishermen who use the harbour opposite the island refer to it as 'Chetin' — and both understand you equally whether you speak of 'Chetigne' or 'Shut-In.'

Chetigne was, acording to the story,[4] the name adopted by the one-time island resident who came to the island during the early Acadian settlement of the Chezzetcook area. Chetigne, we are told, was not the man's real name. His own name, Clairmont, he hid because he was wanted for murder in the Southern United States. Clairmont-Chetigne, so the story goes, pretended to be mute and lived the life of a hermit on the island, with only the music he plucked from his violin and the occasional visits with a small Acadian hoy who showed an aptitude for this instrument, to ease the pain of his self-imposed solitude. In the story it is he who discovers part of the treasure buried years before by pirates.

The island, some say, was once also called Pirates' Island. This name seems apt too since pirates apparently used it as a meeting place as well as a favorite site for burying treasure. Since the land is soft and spongy, producing only grass and other low-lying vegetation, it would be a quick and easy matter to bury treasure on almost any part of the island without noticeably disturbing the ground. Even an astute searcher, unaware of the location, would have trouble finding the buried loot. Moreover on Chetigne, pirates need not have worried about shifting sand and erosion, problems reputedly encountered by those who buried treasure on sandy islands such as Caribou in Pictou County. Chetigne has no sandy coastline; its shore is solid granite.

Still, pirates, like everyone else, must have had an unenviable time getting on and off Chetigne. There are plenty of tales of vessels, some of them pirates', striking or being swept onto the reef joining the island to the mainland. Even local fishermen who do land on this island are leery of it except in the finest weather, and even then keep an apprehensive eye on the tide and currents pulling at the shore and ripping over the reef. Even they cannot always predict the vagaries of nature here, since they are quick to tell how many of the most experienced have been marooned on 'Chetin' by cross currents and rip tides when they have merely put ashore briefly to leave lobster pots or to hunt sea ducks. When even local residents are caught out by these lurking dangers, one can imagine how vulnerable strangers, unaware of such conditions, must have been — particularly when pursued or when confronting fog or storm.

Just as no one is sure about the island's name, no one knows who built the small rough stone house beside the pond, or even who inhabited it over the years. The local people are generally agreed, however, that as it began to fall apart its final use was as a fold for the sheep pastured on the island. All that remains today is an indentation in the ground, seemingly a shallow basement, and piles of stones deposited as the building collapsed.

If the pirates or Clairmont-Chetigne did not build this house, a pilot by the name of Lloyd may have built it — perhaps as long as two hundred years ago. At least, according to contemporary local gossip at Three Fathom Harbour, Mr. Lloyd lived on the island at this time because of his work. He was a pilot for sailing vessels entering Halifax harbour. According to one man, Mr. Lloyd lived on the island so that he could beat his rival to pilot jobs. This rival, Mr. Leslie, lived closer to land on Wedge Island, and by the time he attempted to row out to an anchored ship, Mr. Lloyd would already be on board! Thus Pilot's Island would seem as suitable a name as Pirates' Island.

During these early days, mainlanders often saw a light on the island. At first they assumed that the light was from a lantern in the stone house. Then they grew puzzled by the fact that it was so often seen when no one was known to be on the island. And so mainlanders pondered about the strange light. It was a luminous ghost, some said, for want of a better explanation.

After seeing the island, the logical explanation for this light seems to be that the moon, shining on the pond, reflects light, causing the mainland observer to think that there is a light on the island. (People who are on the island do not, it is said, ever see the light.) What makes this theory of reflected light suspect, however, is the fact that this strange glow, according to old tales (and as recorded in the novel, *Chetigne Island*) appears every Friday. Thus the mysterious light remains just one more peculiarity of this island which has guarded its secrets so closely.

Many years have now passed since human beings have lived in this remote spot. Nowadays fishermen sometimes leave traps there during the lobster season and hunters visit it in the fall. That is all. And so, because men so rarely go to this place, birds — herring gulls — have taken it over. In nesting time it is difficult to move without stepping on an egg or a young bird. These gawky youngsters stand motionless in the long grass, apparently attentive to shrill parental warnings. A visitor, who need only reach down to touch them, can easily understand how Audubon was able to observe and draw the same species with such precision on that other Maritime island[5] so long ago. No other artist's model, shrieked at to hold still, ever kept a pose so well.

Although fascinating, a walk on Chetigne in nesting time is far from peaceful because of the frantic agitation of the parent birds. Screaming vilely, they swoop down with outthrust beaks upon intruders who seem to threaten their young.

Not only human beings are anathema to the gulls. They seem constantly on guard lest the cormorants, or 'shag' as the fishermen call them, who live on nearby Wedge Island, invade their territory. And so the old rivalry, begun by Mr. Lloyd of Chetigne and Mr. Leslie of Wedge, is relived day by day by the contemporary avian inhabitants of these tiny islands.

The birds are now sole guardians of Chetigne Island. Neither rumors of a strange light, buried treasure and pirates, nor evidence of a tumble-down house and former inhabitants disturb them. Huddled close to the ground on wild and stormy days or skimming high above the wild flowers and berries in clear weather, they cannot be lured far from their enchanted island.

The Vesper bell is chiming, and here in sweet Acadie,[6] all is well with the world. The shadows are falling now over the little island, and the strange men who dwelt there have gone to that bourne from which no traveller returns. Afar over the distant iridescent sea, the chimes are pealing, over the sweet meadowlands, the hills and forest aisles.

— Margaret McLaren
Chetigne Island

1. Anthony Lockwood, *A Brief Description of Nova Scotia*, 1818.

2. When Lockwood described this island, he mentioned that it was treed. Once cut or burned, trees would have difficulty getting started again in such a harsh environment. On other islands along this part of the Eastern Shore — Devil's Island, for example, where more

67

recently fire has destroyed the trees — they have not managed to make a comeback either.

3. Neap tide.

4. The novel, *Chetigne Island.*

5. Audubon used the herring gulls on Whitehead Island in the Grand Manan archipelago as the models for his famous drawings of this species when he visited there in 1833. These birds no longer nest on Whitehead Island because of the large increase in human population in recent years. They are keen on having an island mostly to themselves — and in Audubon's time only Mr. Frankland and his family lived on Whitehead.

6. One of the most surprising aspects of Mrs. McLaren's book is her obvious delight in 'Acadie' and 'Acadiens.' Halifax born and bred as she was, she depicts 'Acadie' and its French inhabitants lovingly. But then, of course, her American predecessor Longfellow was a kindred spirit in this regard.

Chapter Six

SCATARIE ISLAND: LOUISBOURG'S OUTPORT AND SABLE ISLAND'S RIVAL

"The Isle of Scatary is suitable only for cod fishery. The situation is one of the best for trade, but, unfortunately, the ports and harbours are not safe. It lies in the sea opposite to Menadou (Main-à-Dieu). It is estimated to be two leagues in length, lying east and west with a breadth, north and south of half a league. Generally speaking the island is a mere rock. The nature of the ground varies, two kinds of soil being found. The one is wet and tenacious the other partakes of the character of marl. It is not by any means wooded, and there is no hard wood on it, neither is there fir or any description of pine suitable for the building of the platforms and scaffoldings that are used on the island. The settlers have to bring their wood from the lands on the river Mire, or from those of the barachois de Catalogne which are near them."

— Sieur de la Roque
Census (1752)

Two miles beyond the nearest mainland harbor, Main-à-Dieu, on Cape Breton's Atlantic coast, lies a rockbound island with a remarkable history. Indeed, the fact that this island, Scatarie, has any recorded history at all — save that relating to shipwrecks — seems on first consideration astonishing, since it is surrounded by extraordinarily

69

dangerous shoals and much of the time is either whipped by rough seas and high winds or shrouded in dense fog. Rocky, boggy, with wind-stunted evergreens its only trees, Scatarie is in nearly every way the antithesis of fertile and sheltered Port Hood Island on Cape Breton's south-western (Northumberland Strait) coast. As a marine hazard Scatarie has been grouped with, and indeed said to rival, such notorious trouble spots as Sable Island, Saint Paul's Island (twelve miles off the northern tip of Cape Breton) and Seal Island (fifteen miles off Cape Sable Island on Nova Scotia's southernmost extremity).[1]

A trip by fishing boat along Scatarie's coast as far as the deteriorating wharf at the north-eastern end does little to dispel fear or convince a newcomer that this was ever a good place to live. For seven miles as the boat skirts the coast it is only just out of reach of the cruel rocks, many of them 'sunkers' (just under the surface) in Scatarie parlance. Yet a considerable number of people lived on this island happily and had a well-established community here long before settlement in more accessible and fertile parts of the Maritime Provinces was ever thought of. For the greater part of two hundred years the population, whether French or English, was stabilized at between one and two hundred, although in 1716 four hundred people lived on Scatarie.[2]

Scatarie's excellent cod fisheries, together with its proximity to the great fortress of Louisbourg, were responsible for the island's early prominence. In the early eighteenth century the ocean around this island teemed with fish. Even in 1740, when Scatarie's population was at its lowest in twenty-five years, due to several successive years of relatively poor catches, six Scatarie schooners marketed 3,600 quintals of cod, and eighteen shallops, 4,500 quintals. Since a quintal is 112 pounds, by our reckoning this would be 907,200 pounds dry weight. According to one British gentleman who wrote a book advocating a British takeover and occupancy of Cape Breton, "...there is no part of the world where more codfish is caught, nor where there is so good convenience for drying it."[3] Indeed, the prosperity of Louisbourg depended on the harvest of cod at Scatarie (fourteen miles distant) and other nearby outports along Cape Breton's south-eastern coast.

Although the early eighteenth century merchants in Louisbourg and Europe made their fortunes from the cod-fish trade, fishermen (some 2,500 of them in and around Louisbourg) risked their lives for a pittance. Not only were most of these men miserably paid for working in a dangerous and uncomfortable environment, but the majority had no home and loving family to return to at the end of hours of cold, wet drudgery.

In all the outport settlements there was a disproportionate number of single men. For instance, the 1716 census of Scatarie records 21 men, 14 women, 46 children, and 319 'hommes compagnons.' So many able-bodied men were needed not only for the actual fishing, but also for all the precise and time-consuming labor involved in preparing cod to meet the high standards of the Mediterranean market. The fish had to be gutted, filleted and salted in the most expert manner as soon as it was caught. Then followed the lengthy process of drying each catch on the flakes, turning the fish every twenty-four hours to insure that both sides cured equally. Even when the catch was on the flakes, the men had to be ready to rush the curing fish under cover before rain or dew could discolor the white flesh and make it unacceptable to the fastidious palates of prospective European buyers.

The 'hommes compagnons,' who constituted more than three-quarters of Scatarie's population at the time of the colony's inception, were merely hired out on the fishing stations where they received a small wage. At night they returned to bleak, unheated bunk houses where they had few possessions other than a change of clothing. Much like their Portuguese and Spanish predecessors of the century before, they stayed for the season — from early spring until just before the drift ice made fishing impossible. They were not colonists. If they had a family in France, they would leave Ile Royale for the harshest part of the winter with one of the last boats taking cod to Mediterranean markets. The following spring they would return to the fishing grounds, but generally with no hope of improvement in wages or opportunities with the passing of years. The dream of acquiring land and fishing stations was as far beyond the reach of most of these men as owning a ranch was for the majority of cowboys in the days of the Old West.

Although some historians have been highly critical of the French regime's inhumane treatment of its fishermen, others have shown that transient workers seem to have been only one group of unintended victims of general administrative mismanagement in France. J.F. McLennan in his book, *Louisbourg*, remarks:

> It is difficult to read the documents from which this narrative has been compiled and not to believe that the wretched state of Isle Royale was owing to incompetence and neglect on the part of the home administration. It is equally difficult to read the accounts of France in the previous score of years, while the kingly sun of the great Louis was descending behind the clouds, all of which tell of hideous poverty, of a stagnant commerce, of an almost naked peasantry suffering from severe winters, from plague and pestilence, of governmental interference which aggravated the miseries of the people, and not to wonder how the ordinary expenses were provided for, how pensions could be allotted or gratuities given to deserving officers, or a new establishment like Louisbourg carried on.[4]

After being reminded by some of the above statements of the dreadful hardships of many of the ordinary people who stayed in France, one can but conclude that transients and settlers alike were better off in the new colony — even in so harsh an environment as Scatarie's. Here at least firewood, fish and game were plentiful and free for those who made the effort to procure them.

From a contemporary vantage point, one can scarcely see how the fisherman's lot improved greatly after the British took over Cape Breton in 1758 — except that from this time on the majority of the fishermen were not transients. The few French who were left after the exodus following the final Louisbourg defeat and the handful of Scots, English, and Irish who gradually settled along this rocky coast were established permanently in their own homes with their families. Nevertheless, by all accounts, the British neglected this whole region for more than half a century after they acquired it. When British merchants finally turned their attention to the fisheries in this part of the world, they did not spend any more time considering the fishermen and their needs than their French predecessors had.

Even early in this century Scatarie's fishermen were hardly well off: they were getting $4.50 a quintal — or .04 cents per pound for dried cod. John Harris, a former island fisherman, recalled one depression winter (1934) when the islanders were in real need. They had run out of food, so some of the men had to make the risky trek over drift ice for emergency supplies.

The drift ice in a more general way contributed to the islanders' difficulties, since it limited their fishing to seven or eight months of the year. Unlike the fishermen of Nova Scotia's South Shore or Fundy coast, fishermen of Scatarie had to haul their boats out of the water between December and April, and even in the fifties, when the last of the islanders left Scatarie, there was still, as Mr. Harris pointed out, "no unemployment insurance to tide fishermen over the months when they could not work."

However, the final blow to island living was advancing technology. By mid twentieth century the old process of salting and drying fish was outdated. Using the ancient and time-consuming methods, islanders could not compete for markets with mainlanders who were by then taking their daily catch fresh to nearby fish plants. Moreover, for islanders who attempted to take the catch in fresh, the extra return trip to the mainland after a day's fishing became an impossible price to pay for island living. The departure of these islanders and their families brought to an end nearly two centuries of community life in a spot which had seemed uninhabitable but became a good place to live because of the day-to-day vigor, valor and generosity of her people. As Edgar Spenser, a former Scatarie Island resident, remarked nostalgically: "Everybody was one person on Scatarie....Everybody that had anything would share with you..."[5]

The French who first settled Scatarie arrived on the island just after 1713 when the Treaty of Utrecht ceded Cape Breton to France — at the time, Louisbourg was being settled as well. Indeed the growth of Scatarie parallels that of Louisbourg, not only because of Scatarie's excellent fisheries, but also because of its strategic importance.

The man most responsible for recognizing this importance and for encouraging the settlement and strengthening of Louisbourg and its outports between 1713 and 1715 was the French Minister of the Marine (the man in charge of colonial development), Louis-Phélypeaux, Comté de Pontchartrain. He made the perspicacious and often-quoted statement that: "If France were to lose this island (Cape Breton) the loss would be an irreparable one, and it would involve the loss of all her holdings in North America." This statement, by the way, was obviously subscribed to by the conquering Wolfe (in 1759) and proved by history correct.

As a consequence of Pontchartrain's immense influence on the initial stages of the development of Louisbourg and its outports, Scatarie was renamed 'Pontchartrain', a designation which survived for some years (usually in conjunction with the original, 'Scatary') even on English maps of Cape Breton such as Thomas Kitchin's. Doubtless the reason Pontchartrain's name held on Scatarie even after the Minister of the Marine lost his influential position in France in 1715 following the death of Louis XIV, had something to do with the fact that he had had a hand in securing for his relative, Jean Phélypeaux, the lucrative sinecure of fishing station owner on this island. Pontchartrain's (Phélypeaux) signature also appears on other early Scatarie island land grants.

By 1726 a large enough population was established here for the Recollets from Louisbourg to consider Scatarie one of three important dependent missions, and in 1734 the island's first church was dedicated — to Saint Catherine. This choice of name for the church lends support to speculations that the island's name is an Indianized version of the Portuguese pronunciation of Saint Catherine. The Portuguese connection with the island was long-standing since they had used much of the south-eastern coast of Cape Breton, including Scatarie, as a seasonal fishing base before the French established Louisbourg. In any case, the island first appeared on a map of 1656 as 'Scatori'. In many eighteenth century French manuscripts and ships' logs the spelling is 'Scatary' or

'Scatory'.

After the first English conquest of Louisbourg in 1745 many of those who had lived on Scatarie returned to France at the same time as Louisbourg's inhabitants. However, there was not the mass exodus from Scatarie that there was from Louisbourg. A core of the permanent community seemed to have escaped deportation. Indeed, Jean-Baptiste Guion, the only Louisbourg resident who managed to remain in the town throughout the English occupation, went to Scatarie in 1746 to take a wife. The marriage was a somewhat unusual one for a straight-laced and conventionally-religious colonial society, since the ceremony was conducted on the island without benefit of the clergy before a group of neighbors. The community was of course hard-pressed to think of a better solution, since all the priests had by this time returned to France. The marriage was finally blessed by the church when the clergy returned to Louisbourg in 1749.

When the Ile Royale colony again came under French control, Scatarie's population remained at about one hundred. These people were landowners and their families; few seasonal workers seemed to have returned. Nevertheless, official recognition of Scatarie's significance in relation to Louisbourg had not diminished since Pontchartrain's time. M. de Chabert hired by the King of France during the years 1750 and 1751 to chart the waters off Cape Breton, said of Scatarie: "This island, situated at the north-easter point of Ile Royal, is the natural landfall for all vessels coming to Louisbourg."[6]

While recognizing Scatarie's significance, M. de Chabert also described the perils attendant on visiting this island. He himself, while on a map-making mission had difficulties getting to the island as well as leaving it. Even while camped for the purpose of taking readings and making notes, his tent was blown over several times. His depiction of a forlorn and even malevolent place, though brief, is somewhat similar to Herman Melville's account, almost a century later of the 'Encantadas' or 'Enchanted' Islands (the Galapagos). Still, unlike Melville's 'Enchantadas,' Scatarie was a much-frequented outpost both before and after the time of M. de Chabert's visit — until 1758, that is. Then with the second English conquest of Louisbourg and a second deportation,

Scatarie, together with most of the rest of Cape Breton, seems to have been forsaken by French and English alike.

Having conquered Louisbourg once and for all, the English were intent on the systematic destruction of all the settlements associated with the Louisbourg Empire. Indeed, a part of the heart-breaking job of destroying these outposts and deporting their residents fell to Wolfe who, with Amherst, had commanded the English force which had finally defeated Louisbourg. In a letter to his father dated August 21, 1758, in Louisbourg, Wolfe wrote ironically: "Sir Charles Hardy and I are preparing to rob the fishermen of their nets and to burn their huts. When the great exploit is at an end (which we reckon will be a month's or five weeks' work), I return to Louisbourg...." And, again from Louisbourg, on September 30 of the same year, he wrote the following words to Major-General Amherst: "Your orders were carried into execution....We have done a great deal of mischief, — spread the terror of His Majesty's arms through the whole gulf; but have added nothing to the reputation of them."[7]

Strategically, the British felt, it was important to rid the Cape Breton coast, and indeed the whole Gulf of Saint Lawrence, of strong French settlements so that they could use this region as a secure base from which to launch an attack on Quebec. Not only were the French colonists deported, but in an attempt to eradicate quickly all memory of the French presence, even some place names were changed — at least temporarily. Thus, briefly, Scatarie lost its centuries-old name, becoming Wolfe Island[8] in honor of the conquering English hero.

Still, the destruction of Scaterie's and other similar settlements must have been a hollow triumph, since in the years following the English victory no settlers hastened to take up the lands which the French had been forced to vacate. Holland, sent out by the British in 1766 and 1767 to map and take stock of their new domains in Cape Breton, came up with an evaluation of Scatarie reminiscent of those written by his French counterparts of the preceding decade, Sieur de la Roque and M. de Chabert — except for the fact that Holland saw only a dead settlement where deserted homes stood next to overgrown gardens:

The Face of this Island (Scatari or Wolfe) is very rocky and barren and the Woods scarce fit for fewel, being nothing, but small Spruce. In the different Coves of this Coast were employed by the French above 200 Shallops in the Fishery, but of a smaller Construction than ordinary as it was usual in Winter to Hawl them on Shore. At How and Baren Coves were some Habitations with Garden Spots and the South East Side is pretty clear, but the Soil produces nothing but Moss and Berries.[9]

Scatarie, as well as the nearby mainland, unlike the fertile lands from which the Acadians in southern Nova Scotia had been driven, would have seemed to prospective newcomers a sterile and hostile environment, and the publication of Holland's findings would only have substantiated such impressions. The slow recovery of the whole region is emphasized by the fact that by 1774 even once proud and populous Louisbourg had only eleven inhabitants.

Apart from steadily accumulating statistics about shipwrecks off its coats, there appear to be no facts recorded about Scatarie between 1766 and 1836 when James Dodd,[10] a veteran of the Royal Navy who had participated in the American War of 1812, moved to the island to take charge of the 'Humane Establishment' — a lifesaving station. After three years in this capacity, Dodd was appointed first keeper of the new light station, built on the northeast point in apparent response to public outcries about the vulnerability of shipping off Scatarie's treacherous and unlit shores.

With the light station established, other families gradually resettled the island, so that by 1869, two years prior to the construction of a second lighthouse on the west end, six families in addition to the superintendent lived on Scatarie. These new settlers were English-speaking, most of them Newfoundlanders, but their lives, inevitably regulated by the tempo of the sea, differed little from those of their French-speaking predecessors. Bringing in the cod, splitting it on the beach, salting, rinsing and drying it, loading it into boats to be sold — the back-breaking work was the same in either language.

Right up to the early decades of the twentieth century, life on Scatarie went on much as it had for a good part of two hundred years. In the first third of this century there were still sixteen or seventeen families who lived on the island year round, fishing and raising a few animals on the side. (Vegetables were almost impossible to bring to maturity because the island's large deer population ate them.) The island people were, by all accounts, a hardy, happy and healthy lot. Even in the early forties twelve families clung tenaciously to island life. They had their own church, a new school (built in 1940) and a Co-operative Society.

After work was finished, they engaged in all sorts of pastimes which they found rewarding: skating or iceboating on the pond in winter, cutting firewood, picking wild berries (particularly bake-apples, cranberries and strawberries which grow in such profusion on this island), hunting (since ducks and deer abound), and even dressing up at Christmas time in mummers' costumes of their own design.

Newfoundlanders who had migrated to Scatarie brought the mumming tradition with them. Three former Scatarie Island residents, Joe, Clem and Mame Spenser, have recalled vividly the way this custom was practised on Scatarie:

Joe: We started about a week before Christmas. We wouldn't buy false faces at all. Get cotton and paint it and make our own faces.

Clem: Some bad faces, too. Scary faces. Used to take a bird and skin it and turn the feathers inside and skin outside and cut holes and paint it, and with the feathers it would be like pimples all over the face.

Joe: Dress up as ugly as we could. Probably ten of us dressed up — and another fellow with a fiddle. Mouth organ. Anything at all. Went to every house on the island. Dance. Wouldn't sing very much because they'd know your voice. When you're a mummer you try to talk different than you used to talk. We'd have great times. They'd have to guess you. Try to get your shape... Have to figure out who you'd be. Every Christmas. Come a heavy snowstorm then we wouldn't go — but clear of that. Dancing and singing, lots of booze around.

Mame: We just sang Christmas songs, and some would sing the odd hymn and some would sing little rhymes — not too much. Afraid if you sang too much they'd catch on.

Such descriptions are reminiscent of the pace and focus of life which Thomas Hardy conjures up in his nineteenth century novels of life on Egdon Heath. Similarities between residents of Egdon Heath and those of Scatarie are heightened by the way in which both groups of people subscribe to their own regional bland of folklore and superstition. The ghosts of Scatarie are particularly distinctive and fall into two categories: those which are supposed to have survived from the time of the French occupation and those connected with the victims of marine disasters.

Former residents, Abbie and Edgar Spenser, have related how the ghosts of the French settlers returned to haunt Scatarie:

Abbie: There was a French burying ground under our house. When we'd wake up in the morning the bed would be shaking for no reason. Be going to talk on the telephone some days, the telephone be shaking in your hand. This kind of stuff. Then we'd hear oil barrels roll.

Edgar: We were sitting down one time and everything upstairs was cleaned up. And it was just as though somebody tipped an oil barrel on its side and rolled it across. And there was two women there talking to me. I said to one, 'What was that?' When they left I went upstairs. There wasn't a dust moved. We knew it must be a French burying ground because it was a clear place where I built the house. The French lived out there on Scatarie. You go over the hills, you see the stone foundations where they had their houses.

Scatari was a good harbour. There's a place off Scatari called Hay Island. There's a bar that ran across. Well that was all land when the French were here. When you came in the harbour you came straight in — beautiful harbour. And Power's Island — there's a pond and there was an island and the beach ran along this way. And there was an old tree on this island — standing up — a dead tree. And one day brother Willy — he's twelve years older than me — he was just a little fellow — he saw a French shallop come in — you know what a French shallop was — a three master like. She came in and she anchored in the harbour. And they came ashore in a boat. And they brought an old man ashore. And they led him up to this island. And they went back and went aboard. Next morning when the people got up, that tree was torn down. Big hole dug under the tree. The ship was gone.

Edgar Spenser had another story about a ghost from the French period:

I was down after a load of rum — watching for them to land it. Right dark — and I was standing up. All at once I felt like there was someone behind me. So I turned around to look. Seen a brown shadow....fade like that. And that's what they used to bury them in — brown habits.... The Catholic people. Just like a shroud you know.

John Harris, now a Louisbourg resident, tells one of the most memorable tales of the surviving French presence on Scatarie:

Oh yes, there's gold on the island all right, lots of it in different places...been there from the time when the French were having problems with the English here at Louisbourg. It's been there for a long time now, but no one on Scatarie ever got any of it. No one dared to dig it up. This was because they buried the gold each time with a corpse on top, so that before you'd get to the gold you'd be face to face with a skeleton.... No. No one on Scatarie ever saw any of that gold. They didn't think it worth the risk.

Most frequent island revenants, however, were shipwrecked mariners. Bodies were frequently washed ashore.

Indeed one fisherman recalls how after the *Callisto* ran aground on Point Nova in April, 1929, islanders were picking up bodies all summer on Scatarie's beaches.

One favorite story concerns the ghost of a man from the *Ringhorn* which was lost August 7, 1926, off Scatarie. Some four or five months after this disaster, an islander was over on the south side of the island hewing out a log. Becoming aware of someone behind him, he straightened up. The intruder disappeared at once, and the islander continued his work. However, when this had happened four or five times, the hewer abandoned his log and hurried home.

On another occasion after the *Ringhorn* went ashore, two men, Bill Spenser and Anthony Wadden, were on their way to Southern Point before daybreak to shoot ducks when, on reaching Sandy Cove, they heard a bell ringing in the woods. They could not believe their ears since they were well aware that there could not be a bell anywhere nearby.

Yet even before the *Ringhorn* sank, strange presages of disaster were observed. Here is Edgar Spenser's account:

> And the night the *Ringhorn* went ashore, we were sitting down chewing the bone, talking, and all the covers on the stove turned bottom up — had six covers on it. They all turned bottom up. That's hard to believe.

and

> I heard that somebody at Southern Point stayed out there alone. He was asleep. It come up a big storm — rain, blowing. About 2 o'clock in the morning the camp door opened. In walked eight or nine men with their oilcloths on. And they sat around the fire. And after a while he kind of rubbed his eyes — and there was no one there. Two days afterward there was a ship come ashore — nine men lost.

Some of the men who drowned and were washed ashore on Scatarie were buried there in unmarked graves, whereas others were taken to the mainland for burial; but near the northeastern light four brightly painted white crosses stand out against the windswept grass as if they had been placed there yesterday. The government maintains these graves, yet no names appear on or near the crosses. The lightkeeper or any former islander will tell you that they mark the burial sites of four men who drifted ashore when their boat was torpedoed off Scatarie during the first world war. The light keepers at the time heard cries in the night, but were unable to find the men in the darkness. By morning the strangers lay dead on the shore.

Since ships have been going down off Scatarie with great regularity for at least three centuries, inevitably interest has been shown in the cargoes of some of these vessels. The cargoes which caught most peoples' attention were, of course, gold — gold shipped to Louisbourg to meet the payroll and lost on the shoals close to their destination. Since captains headed for Louisbourg steered for the most striking landmark on that part of the coast — the triangular island of Scatarie — and since too often the island was shrouded in fog, many ships ran onto the reefs and shoals which extend at least a mile from Scatarie in every direction.

Divers have been willing to brave all the perils of working in these waters for the riches they hope to come up with. They are doubtless spurred on by local gossip concerning the vast numbers of gold coins found between Louisbourg and Main-à-Dieu several years ago. Yet who knows what has been found off Scatarie itself; the treasure seekers have not been quick to say. An indication that they have not come up totally empty-handed is that every summer divers are at work between Hay Island[11] (an islet just off Scatarie) and Scatarie with the dawn to dusk enthusiasm of gold miners who have just struck pay dirt. Still these men, like the adventurers of the Yukon gold rush who braved comparable environmental hazards, seem less obviously content with the results of their labors than the people who were not transients here and who struggled so hard simply to survive.

On an island where courage and endurance were taken for granted in accomplishing everyday routines, an individual had to demonstrate exceptional heroism to stand out. However, one Scatarie island resident who managed to impress islanders and mainlanders alike with her extraordinary valor and stamina was a woman, Mrs. Eliza

Campbell, keeper of the western light for twenty-one years. When her husband, former keeper of this light, was drowned off Scatarie in 1942, Mrs. Campbell simply took over the job. Not only did she have the responsibility for maintaining the light, but for bringing up her three children. Since the western light was more than four miles from school or neighbors, Mrs. Campbell taught the children herself; and, according to one former islander, "They got a good education, because Mrs. Campbell was a well-educated lady. She read a lot — books and magazines like *Time*. Let me tell you, she knew what was going on in the world!"

Teacher, nurse, and keeper of the light, Mrs. Campbell was never known to weaken — even after one of her sons perished as her husband had in a small boat just off Scatarie. Until she retired, when she moved reluctantly to Main-à-Dieu, she maintained that she loved her life and work on Scatarie.

Since the human exodus from Scatarie, new creatures have been introduced to this island. Like the last wave of human migrants, these new immigrants — willow grouse, ptarmigan and arctic hare — were brought from Newfoundland and expected to adapt promptly to Scatarie because of the similarity in climate and vegetation on these two islands. However, as has been demonstrated all over the world, the fate of transplanted creatures is difficult to predict.

Contrary to the expectations of the wildlife scientists, these new species did not thrive on Scatarie. Foxes, apparently unknown on the island since the days of the Louisbourg empire, when both they and the partridges they sometimes hunted were reputed to be abundant, they must have got wind of the exotic delicacies in store for them if they crossed from the mainland on the drift ice. However they got there, foxes are now firmly established on Scatarie, and neither willow grouse nor arctic hare are to be seen. As for the ptarmigans, some former islanders claim that they have flown to the mainland — thus showing themselves to be quite as mobile and resourceful as their human predecessors.

And so Scatarie impassively awaits its next immigrants who will come when the time is ripe — perhaps in ten years, perhaps in a hundred. Whenever they arrive they are unlikely to find Scatarie greatly changed from the way the Portuguese sailors saw it in the seventeenth century, the first French immigrants early in the eighteenth, or James Dodd, lighthousekeeper, in the nineteenth. Only a few rotting rail fences along one cliff, several old foundations, the deteriorating wharf, the light station and the narrow road leading to it attest to the fact that human beings have lived here.

1. "Scatarie Island, for which vessels bound from England to our possessions in North America, usually shape their course lies a few miles from Mira Bay, on the south-east coast of Cape Breton. A light-house should for mere humanity sake be erected on this island, and I would entreat the attention of the patriotic brethren of the Trinity House, to the following facts obtained from a Halifax paper: — 'If we look to the comparative loss of life and property in these places, we shall not find that on Scatarie and St. Paul's to be trifling. The loss at the Isle of Sable, in the aggregate, during twenty-one years from 1806 to 1827 was about thirty-five vessels — two indeed of these were frigates, besides several ships and brigs; but great part of them schooners and fishing vessels. In the vicinity of St. Paul's and Scatarie, there have been in 1832, three ships, one barque, eight brigs and several small vessels, in all about 3,000 wrecked tons; and in 1833, four ships, four brigs and two schooners, near 2,800 tons and containing upward of 600 souls. How many more have suffered in these places, and at the Isle of Sable, who can tell. Here is a summary of the known loss in two years; but if the estimate be correct that the loss of shipping in the vicinity of St. Paul's and Scatarie, has been for the last twenty years about 2,000 tons per annum, how awfully great must be the loss from first to last, as in such cases in twenty years about 40,000 tons of shipping must have been wrecked in these two places, which is a far greater loss than at the Isle of Sable in the same given period. A recent calculation estimates the loss of life on these rocks during the past years at upwards of 1000." (*History of Nova Scotia*, Robert Montgomery Martin, 1837, pp. 88 and 89.)

2. In this same census the population of Louisbourg was designated as five hundred and sixty-four.

3. Bollen, W., *The Importance and Advantage of Cape Breton*, p. 52.

4. McLennan, J.S., *Louisbourg*, The Book Room, Halifax, 1979 (first published by Macmillan in 1918), p. 39.

5. This quotation and others by the Spensers in this chapter are from "Remembering Life on Scatarie Island", *Cape Breton Magazine*, No. 14, August, 1976, pp. 27-32.

6. Chabert, M. de, *Voyage fait par ordre du roi en 1750 et 1751 dans l'Amérique Septentrionale,* Johnson Reprint Corporation, Mouton and Co., N.Y., 1966, p. 41. (The translation is mine).

7. Willson, Beckles, *The Life and letters of James Wolfe,* Heinemann, London, 1909, pp. 396 and 397.

8. See Shelburne Papers, Vol. 77, 1767 — letter from George d'Erbage in Quebec to the Earl of Shelburne. In this letter he recounts that the French once had 200 shallops on Scatarie (Wolfe) and that the English could reasonably expect to maintain a similar number of fishing vessels on this island. Holland's 1766-67 study makes the same statement.

9. *Holland's Description of Cape Breton Island,* Complied by D. C. Harvey, Public Archives of Nova Scotia, 1935, p.79.

10. James Dodd (1795-1855) was a son of the second Chief Justice of Cape Breton. Since Chief Justice A.C. Dodd was so important a man, his Sydney house by all accounts so well-appointed and the focus of so many prestigious social gatherings of Nova Scotia's elite, one wonders how two of his sons could bring themselves to leave the elegance and lustre of such privileged surroundings for the harsh, solitary and dangerous life of superintendent on several of the world's most feared islands — Scatarie and Sable. (Philip Dodd, James' younger Brother, was

superintendent on Sable Island for eighteen years, during which time, according to one newspaper report, he did not once leave the island!)

11. 'Ile de la Tremblade' in the time of the Louisbourg empire.

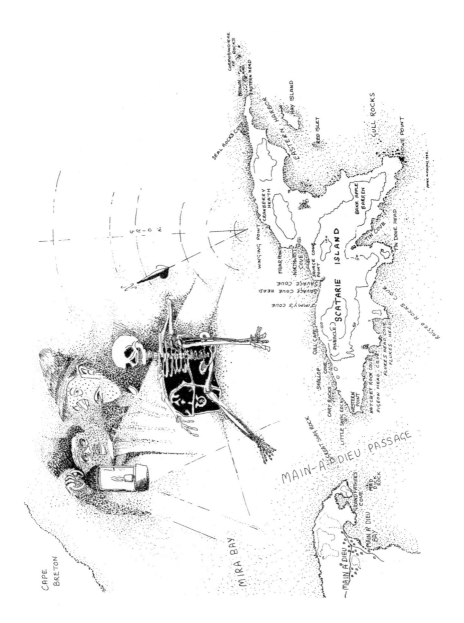

87

Chapter Seven

PICTOU ISLAND:
THE SLUMBERING LEVIATHAN

"Pictou Island, the centre of which has considerable elevation, does not look unlike some monster of the deep, enjoying his slumbers in the sun."

— Joseph Howe, 1828
Travel Sketches of Nova Scotia
(Western and Eastern Rambles)

In the summer of 1828 when Joseph Howe made this passing remark about Pictou Island, he was apparently content to view it from the distant security of the mainland where he could count on finding comfortable inns and hearty eating houses after a day's rambles. He seems to have been less interested in the island than several of his equally famous predecessors had been.

Nicholas Denys, the great explorer, and DesBarres, the famous cartographer (*The Atlantic Neptune*, 1760) had both charted the waters around Pictou Island; and Colonel Alexander McNutt, the somewhat notorious land speculator, had actually been granted the island in 1761 as part of 100,000 acres ceded to him in Pictou County.[1] Yet, despite these brushes with the great and near great, the island seems really to have slumbered until just prior to Howe's rambles in Pictou County. Although Howe seems unaware of it, this was the

NORTHUMBERLAND STRAITS

FERRY TO WOOD POINT P.E.I.

PICTOU ISLAND

BIG CARIBOU ISLAND

CARIBOU HARBOR

LITTLE CARIBOU ISLAND

CRAHAME PT.

LOGAN PT.

TOWN OF PICTOU

PICTOU LANDING

WEST RIVER

MERIGOMISH HARBOR

LITTLE HARBOR

Scale: Approx. 1.5 in. to 1 mile
PETER MITCHAM 1982

time of the great awakening on Pictou Island. Scots, some of them descendants of the first Pictou County immigrants who had arrived on the *Hector* fifty years earlier, had by 1828 taken firm root in the island soil. During the next century they and their sturdy and independent offspring made Pictou Island into a thriving and busy community.[2]

Howe's remark better fits our time, for it is now, in the twentieth century, that the island seems to have slipped back to sleep. The contemporary traveller, zooming along the Gulf Shore road at a speed Howe never dreamed of, is unlikely even to spot the island. If he were to catch sight of it, he would probably be as reluctant as Howe to leave the beaten track. And why indeed should the idea even cross his mind? Pictou Island is so far offshore that, viewed from the mainland, its outlines are usually blurred. It could be dismissed as a mirage if the traveller did not have a map at hand. And anyway, what is over there? Why bother to go? Even a nearby mainlander would be hard-pressed to answer these questions, since chances are he has never been there and has little inclination to go.

His indifference is not surprising. Pictou Island is almost nine miles from the town of Pictou, and about seven from the nearest point of land — Caribou. It is well outside the arms of any sheltering bay, which means that boats sometimes have difficulty reaching it even in summer and cannot get there at all in the dead of winter. The island has no inns, no restaurants, no camping grounds, no car ferry — no, not even a proper store! A part-time store opens only in the evenings and on weekends when the owner is home from his main occupation — fishing.

Yet, all these superficial inconveniences aside, the romantically-inclined visitor who chances to set foot on Pictou Island on a sunny midsummer day will not understand why such an enchanting isle is all but abandoned. The few houses which are still occupied look attractive and well cared for. The spellbinding beauty of the rocky northern coast, the white sand beaches, the reputed productivity of the land, seem not to jibe with the irrefutable evidence of many abandoned and disintegrating houses, a sagging wharf and unworked land. Why, he ponders, has the population of this island, the largest

(6 miles long, 2 miles wide, 2,900 acres) of the Northumberland Strait islands except Prince Edward Island,[3] shrunk during the last century from about 400 to the present 20?

A realist soon has the answers. The island has no electricity, no extensive fishing industry, no regular year-round transportation — and no practical way of acquiring them. Has Pictou Island been victimized? is the next question. After all, smaller Nova Scotia islands such as Brier, the Tancooks, and even Ironbound have none of these problems and are obviously thriving. Having given the question some consideration, the objective observer must conclude that no one is really to blame, that Pictou Island's geographical situation is the key to its predicament.

Unlike Brier or the Tancooks, Pictou is too far from the mainland to be supplied easily with power. Running a cable under the ocean from the nearest point of land some seven miles away would be too expensive, particularly in view of the gradual decline in the island's fishery. Whereas fishing off Briar and the Tancooks is still big business for many, fishing off Pictou supports only a few. A contemporary observer can hardly imagine that fifty years ago thirty workers staffed a thriving fish-packing plant on the north shore of Pictou Island. No sign of it remains today.

Perhaps the greatest difficulty which besets Pictou Island residents, and which is not a problem on such islands as Brier and Tancook, is the fact that Pictou Island cannot be reached year-round by boat. Although the eight months of the year fishing boats ply back and forth from island to mainland, for much of the other four months they are prevented from making the crossing because of ice in the Straits. The ice, moreover, is usually not consistently thick enough and stationary enough so that snowmobiles or other overland winter vehicles can be relied on for regular service.

Permanent residents of this island just have to face the fact that for about four months of the year, they are, to some considerable extent, marooned. Indeed, they face problems almost identical to those of residents on some remote arctic islands; and, as on some of these arctic islands, light planes now land on the gravel road which runs some five miles down the middle of the island. Weather permitting, the planes deliver mail twice weekly and make emergency evacuations. Apart from these weekly flights, the elemental dangers and difficulties of life on Pictou Island are much as they have always been. Facing such difficulties calls for a special breed of people — and Pictou Island has produced it. Nearly everyone who lives on this island or has ever lived there for long has a quiet and justifiable sense of pride in this island and in the accumulated exploits of its people. The surrounding sea has provided the stage on which so many of the real life dramas of Pictou islanders have been enacted.

One of the lighter dramas which still stirs the islanders' imaginations concerns a Pictou Island hockey team. The year was 1912. Arrangements had been made for the islanders to play the mainlanders. When the day of the match arrived, the islanders were faced with a not unfamiliar winter problem: How to get to the mainland? During the night the ice had shifted and subsequently large patches of open water were clearly visible, separating stretches of ice. The obvious solution was to concede the game. This, the Pictou Island boys were not prepared to do. So, nothing daunted by nine miles of open water, ice, and floating ice cakes which separated the team from their opponents, they threw their skates and gear into a small boat and pushed off from the island. In open water they rowed; on the ice they ran, pushing or pulling the boat. In this manner they not only arrived on the mainland in time for the game — but they won the game! That night, travelling in the same way as they had come, they returned to the island. Teams the world over may boast of their 'esprit de corps' and achievements, but few can top this feat of the Pictou Island boys.

A second tale of a winter's crossing demonstrates the same sort of daring do. One winter's day a Pictou Island man started off across the ice to purchase groceries on the mainland. The trip over with horse and sleigh was uneventful. After making his purchases, he set off for home about dusk. Then, half way to the island, his horse stopped before a rift in the ice. Several feet of open water flowed between him and the ice on the other side.

Instead of turning back when confronted with this horrifying sight, he calmly unhitched the horse and dragged the sleigh to the edge of the ice, pushing it across the rift until it reached the ice on the other side. Then, strapping the groceries to his horse, he rode it across the 'bridge.' Without incident he galloped the rest of the way home on unbroken ice.

Another winter drama did not end so well. About a century ago — on November 15, 1884 — a steamer, the *Inverault* foundered in a gale off Seal Rock on the northern side of the island. Several Pictou Island men saw the vessel's predicament and set out to rescue survivors. Although they did rescue many, eight men, including one of the island rescuers, lost their lives.

This particular tragedy was commemorated by several ballads written by Pictou's best-known poet of this time, Robert Murdoch. Murdoch, who wrote four poems about this disaster and its Pictou Island heroes, was perhaps obsessed by the occurrence because his own grandfather had perished some years earlier off this island while fishing.

Fortunately, not all the colorful accounts of courage and persistence belong to the distant past. Recently, in the last six or seven years, a few newcomers have made the island their home. The most stubborn have shown their determination to stay and make a place for themselves. Several have proved themselves worthy of their predecessors.

One of these was at first dismissed as being simply a 'foreigner.' Not only did he not hail from Pictou County, but he was not even from Nova Scotia. He came, it turned out, from New Brunswick! This fact, coupled with the rumor that he had been a "college fella," made him suspect among the rugged fishermen, mostly lifelong residents of the island, or at least Pictonians, among whom he had elected to live and work.

After doing their best to dissuade him from a vocation which they judged to be beyond his capabilities and training, they apparently settled back into their usual routines to await the, to them, obvious outcome of the newcomer's foolhardy determination to be a fisherman.

Their prophecies of disaster — of demise or departure — seemed about to be fulfilled in short order. In his handling of the boat, his unfamiliarity with the ways of the sea and the fish, the young man soon proved to be every bit as inept as they had anticipated. Quietly they waited for him to give up, as time after time they towed the pigheaded stranger back to the wharf after finding him lost in the fog or his boat swamped in heavy seas.

Still, they had reckoned without his tenacity. He seemed absolutely determined to do or die — and he did not die. He fishes now with the best of them, and is reputed by his peers to be as good a fisherman as if he had been trained up to the life from childhood.

Not all the tales about this island and her people have to do with the sea, and not all are so easily verified as the ones just related. One story, told by an elderly gentleman, a former island resident, is very strange. This is what he said:

"You know that pond on the south side of the island? ...In the last dip before you're out on the shore? Well, as you know, it's the only pond on the island, and quite a size if you take in all the boggy land around it, thick as it is with cattails and that tall, marsh grass. Every winter during my time and before my time the men used to cut ice off that pond to put into the ice houses, and of course the youngsters skated on it. In later summer the cranberries grew thick alongside it. The girls used to spend hours picking them.... But I'm getting away from the story....

"Anyway, in my father's time — the pond was on his land — folks started noticing early one summer how the grass and cattails was all beat down, just as if something heavy had been dragged time and again through it. What was strange was that there weren't any footprints, no hoof marks from cattle or sheep either — nothing to give a clue. Everyone started speculating, but no one came up with any very bright ideas. Then one night after supper when the chores was done and some of the boys got to talking, they figured they'd just take a walk down through the woods and have another look at the pond and the beat-down grass. The boys were laughing and joking. 'Must be some strange monster, come from the sea, that's got into our pond and's making them markings,' they kidded.

"Well, instead of just standing at the edge of the woods and staring as they'd done before, they set off through the grass and reeds to have a closer look. Mostly they could see pretty well where they was going on account of the way the grass was

flattened.

"Then all of a sudden the fellow in front stopped dead, and the next moment he was backpeddling so fast that the boys behind him went down like ninepins. When they picked themselves up, some of them claimed they'd seen a huge fat snake, a sort of serpent monster, they said. My father said later, when he got his breath back, that he saw it all stretched out to about nine feet.

"Well, they all retreated right smart back through the woods, and, when they got into the house, shut the door tight. For the first time ever, they wished they could lock up. It was almost dark by now, so they lit the oil lamp and sat down to plan how to get rid of the monster. An island's too close quarters to think of sharing it with a creature like that.

"The long and short of it was that they decided to hold off till morning, so they could see what they was about, and then attack. They planned to surround the pond and set fire to all the grass — much of it still dry, last year's dead stuff.

"Bleary-eyed and stiff in the joints after a night of keeping watch and thinking, the boys set off at dawn, and, using lots of oil to make sure the fire took, ringed the swamp and pond with fires. They got back into the woods and watched, but couldn't see nothin' 'cept smoke. Later that morning when she was all burned out, they went back down there. There wasn't no monster, nor any corpse either. But they must've got rid of her, 'cause no one's seen hide nor hair of her since.' "

Another imagination-stretching tale of this island concerns the ubiquitous burning ghost ship of the Northumberland Straits. According to the legend, a woman in white was seen now and then walking from the eastern tip of Pictou Island towards a ball of fire which was clearly visible in the water. As she moved closer, the ball of fire was said to turn into a sailing ship in flames. Almost as soon as the woman disappeared into the flaming vessel, it sank.

About the time the woman in white took her last walk to the phantom ship and the monster disappeared — some fifty years ago, according to local reckoning — Pictou Island was at last linked to mainland Nova Scotia and the rest of the world by the installation of telephones. This service was long overdue, the islanders felt. After all, they had waited almost fifty years longer than their counterparts of Briar Island and Grand Manan for their telephones.

The advent of the telephone meant the end of an unusual way of communicating with the mainland. To indicate emergencies — to tell of severe illnesses or death — islanders had used gas lamps to flash signals. If the visibility was poor, the distress signals could not of course be seen. However, if they were spotted, a boat would then be dispatched from a mainland harbour. The boat would set out for the island and proceed until ice made progress impossible. Then the boat's crew would drop anchor and wait for the islanders to come out to them.

When the islanders spotted the boat, they would put the sick or injured person into an open, horse-drawn sleigh and proceed cautiously onto the ice. When they reached thinner ice, they would unhitch the horse and substitute men between the shafts. They would pull the sleigh still closer to the edge of the ice and the waiting boat. Then, when even this procedure seemed too dangerous, the men would abandon the sleigh and carry the casualty over the last stretch of thin ice.

Although contemporary island telephones appear to be just like those on the mainland, there is a difference. The power for the island's telephones is wind generated. The shiny metal windmill, looking like an experimental sculpture on loan from the Museum of Modern Art, seems strangely out of place in the middle of a hayfield, between the white clapboard church and an old farmhouse.

The link between this island and the mainland is not merely mechanical. There is no denying the strong emotional and environmental bonds between Pictou Island and the rest of Pictou County. Scots have set the tone and pattern of life on both mainland and island. Indeed, the lilting highland voices, sheep-covered hillsides, a close focus on family, hard work and education, an initial wariness with strangers, and a warm-hearted hospitality for friends are almost enough to persuade the visitor that he is in Scotland — in Pitlochry or Kingussie. The names — MacMillan, Rankin, MacDonald, McCullough, Campbell, Cameron, Patterson — only accentuate this impression.

Despite this obvious kinship, former islanders (and there are many of them) who have moved to the mainland for practical considerations — their children's schooling, for instance — invariably regret having left their island. The tranquility of woods and meadows, the exuberance of the seals cavorting just off Seal Rock, the blue expanse of summer ocean stretching to limitless horizons, the gatherings of friends and neighbors at the wharf to meet Charlie's boat, these rarely have their mainland counterparts for former islanders. Most think that it is now too late for them to return to live on this island. "The best that one can hope for," a former island teacher remarked, "is to come to rest at last in the peaceful island cemetery":

some day
when I have had enough
of planting and of harvesting
I shall be content
to lie down forever
in the light velvet earth
beneath the sweet wild grasses
and whispering poplars
where I can listen
on hot still days
to the bees milking the clover
and on fierce stormy ones
to the sea pounding
the northern cliffs

in this island cemetery
near
— though not close-crowded —
to kindred souls
I shall rest
far from the smell of steaming asphalt
and the whine of intercity jets.[4]

1   McNutt had to relinquish this island for the same reason
that he had to give up other land claims throughout Nova

Scotia; namely, because he failed to bring in a sufficient number of settlers and establish them on the land. Then, almost fifty years later, in 1809, Pictou Island was again part of a land grant. This time the grantee was Sir Alexander Cochrane, who was responsible for having the island surveyed. Cochrane too was instrumental in settling three families on the south side of the island and in opening stone quarries.

2. In 1823 Pictou Island had a population of 59. By 1887, there were twenty-seven farms on the island.

3. And Merigomish Island, which is now linked to the mainland by a sand bar.

4. First published in *Bluenose*, 1980.

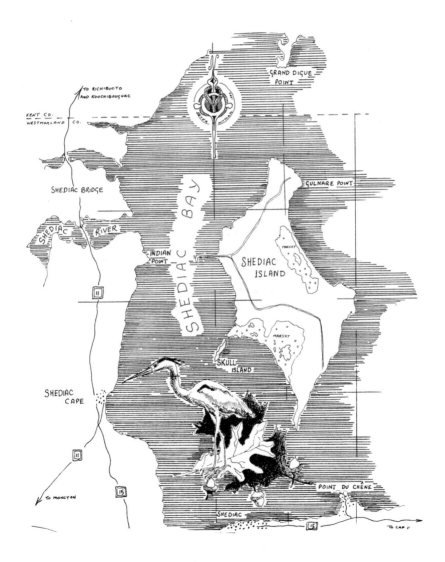

To RICHIBUCTO
AND KOUCHIBOUGUAC

GRAND DIGUE
POINT

KENT CO.
WESTMORLAND CO.

SHEDIAC BRIDGE

GULNARE POINT

SHEDIAC RIVER

SHEDIAC BAY

INDIAN POINT

SHEDIAC ISLAND

MARSHY

MARSHY

SKULL ISLAND

SHEDIAC CAPE

POINT DU CHÊNE

To MONCTON

SHEDIAC

To CAP ?

Chapter Eight
SHEDIAC ISLAND:
HOME OF THE HERONS

Shediac Island is essentially an overgrown sand bar. Stretching nearly two miles across the entrance to Shediac Bay, it is a beautiful and vulnerable spot. With its strong new growth of trees and abundant bird population, this island is a naturalist's dream come true.

Without human inhabitants for the last thirty-five years, Shediac Island has reverted quickly to its natural state. Today no trace remains of the dwellings of the seventeen families (sixteen of them Acadian), seemingly so permanently established here at the beginning of this century.

Apart from the fact that many of the trees are new growth, this island must not look so different from the way it appeared when Nicholas Denys first sailed by it in the seventeenth century or when Governor Wentworth dropped anchor off it and DesBarres first put it on his charts in the eighteenth. Miraculously, even the oaks — which gave the opposite point (Pointe-du-Chêne) its name, and which have long since disappeared from there as elsewhere along the coast — have not died out on the island. Visiting this tiny unspoiled kingdom makes one realize how breathtakingly beautiful and rich in life this whole stretch of coastline must have been before our forebearers cut the pines and oaks to Governor Wentworth's specifications, destroyed hundreds and thousands of sea birds for food and fun, and ringed the shore with chains of wooden cottages. No wonder that Denys, some three hundred years ago, called part of the mainland and one of the islands not far above Shediac, 'Cocagne', which translated into English means 'Utopia'!

A close look at Shediac Island also alerts the visitor to the fragility of this particular environment and the vulnerability of its non-human population. "This island could disappear next week if people aren't more careful," a Shediac man who loves the island remarked thoughtfully. "It wouldn't take much. Just one of those campfires out of hand sweeping across the island, followed by a week or so of storms and high tides, could do it. The island's so low and there's no rock base. Only the trees anchor it."

Anyone who doubts the truth of these comments need not look farther than Little Shediac Island (sometimes called Indian or Skull Island) to realize that he is right. This minute island is at low tide linked to the larger island by an umbilical cord, a thin sand bar. Despite its protected situation in the lee of the larger island, Little Shediac grows smaller every year. Long denuded of trees, its banks are steadily eroding. In a few years it will be washed away. Already the sea has swallowed what remained at the turn of this century of an old Indian fort here.

But why, you may wonder, did human beings abandon Shediac Island — particularly in view of its great beauty and proximity to the town? Partly for the same reasons they have left other offshore islands: they wanted the newly-obtainable conveniences found only on the mainland. It was all very well to live on an island when mainland and island were, by our present standards, both inconvenient. Indeed, up to the early years of this century, islanders often thought themselves better off than their mainland friends and relatives. In summer the islanders' boats were obviously a much quicker, smoother and cleaner way to travel than the mainlanders' dusty and bumpy horse-drawn carts or wagons — and in winter everyone, on island and mainland alike, was snowed in or icebound.

But once cars became commonplace, roads relatively smooth, and snowplows capable of clearing the winter roads; once movie theatres and hospitals were within reach of most mainlanders, islanders felt left out of the mainstream of life.

They embarked for the mainland where electricity, the telephone, the railway, schools, hospitals, churches and stores were all within reach.

But there were other reasons too. Shediac Island, like other Northumberland Strait islands, was an especially inconvenient — dangerous even — place to live when the ice was unsafe. Even half a mile is a long way when shifting ice cakes or soft grey patches of ice lie between you and your mainland destination. . . . One by one the families left the island. . . . School closed. . . . A little girl, Annie Robinson, the lighthouse keeper's daughter, fell through the ice and drowned on her way to school on the mainland. . . . A woman lay dying of cancer with three small boys to look after while her husband went across the ice for the doctor. The neighbors had already moved away. No one was nearby to lend a hand. . . .

"It's all right to take a chance ourselves, but not risk our kids' lives....It's time to move," was murmured across the island. The lighthouse, seemingly a fixture on this island, was shut down and burned — and with the demise of the lighthouse, that sustaining beacon of island life, the last islanders to consider Shediac Island home — the Clements and the Fougères — packed their belongings, dragged the moveable parts of their dwellings across the ice to Pointe du Chêne and struggled to put down new roots there.

Still, apart from all these difficulties, perhaps the greatest deterrent to human residency on Shediac Island has always been the mosquitoes and black flies. The swamp and ponds which cover much of the island seem to provide these creatures with an ideal habitat. They are really menacing, more voracious even than their notorious arctic cousins, and the visitor is hard-pressed to imagine how the islanders managed to live with them for five months each year and keep their sanity. A few hours at a time would drive most people to the brink of madness. Since these rapacious predators seem impervious to even the most touted contemporary insect repellents, how the islanders coped with these pests so long before the invention of insectifuges is impossible to imagine. Former islanders tell of the priest's coming to exorcise these demonic creatures, and of ensuing periods of temporary relief. But the flies and mosquitoes always returned.

For the island's present inhabitants — birds of countless species — these clouds of insects are not pests. Indeed, they provide the birds with a wonderful supply of fast food. And when sated with these delicacies, herons, terns and gulls join sandpipers on the shore or in the shallows for a fish fry. Day after day on the hot midsummer sand the tiny caplin toss and glisten like smelts flipped in a frying pan. Every bird has more than he can eat. As one observant individual remarked: "It's the only place where I've seen gulls unable to choke down another morsel. I've seen them turn away from the caplin looking ill, like overfed travellers waddling away from an all-you-can-eat Howard Johnson fish fry."

Not all the island's birds are so gregarious and noisy as the feasting gulls, sandpipers and terns — and not all are drawn daily to the crowded bar. Like their human counterparts elsewhere, the birds here differ greatly from one another in both habits and habitats. Near shore, though seemingly as far away as they can get from the raucous crowds, family groups of scoters (coots) feed quietly and companionably. If an intruder disturbs them, with one accord they lift their sleek black bodies half out of the water and plane across its surface with the speed and finesse of accomplished water skiers. Once they feel that they have left the troublemaker behind, swamped in their wakes, they settle down again without so much as a backward glance.

More solitary and private is the kingfisher, glimpsed by chance as he dives for fish from the branches overhanging a clear pool, or the hawk who sits in the tall tree above the pond, seemingly meditating upon lofty matters.

Yet it is the herons who dominate this island. One or two herons provide a thrilling spectacle for bird lovers anywhere, but dozens of great blue herons! ... All together! The sight is breath-taking! Unbelievable! Nevertheless, this is the spectacle which overwhelms the newcomer here. The tall black spruces above the marsh in the centre of the island are their nesting places.

Graceful as these large birds seem when flying or standing in shallow water, in the treetops their extraordinarily long legs and great bodies appear strangely out of place. The onlooker might well assume that these birds, like incredible creatures from a Lewis Carrol or Dr. Seuss book, had drunk a magic potion which had made them too large for their perches. However, like all enchanted beings, they seem invulnerable to commonplace rules — and so they do not fall. Summer after summer these great and mysterious creatures return to preside over their tranquil island, to live at peace with the other creatures, and perhaps even to commune with the ghosts of former islanders — French, English and Indian.

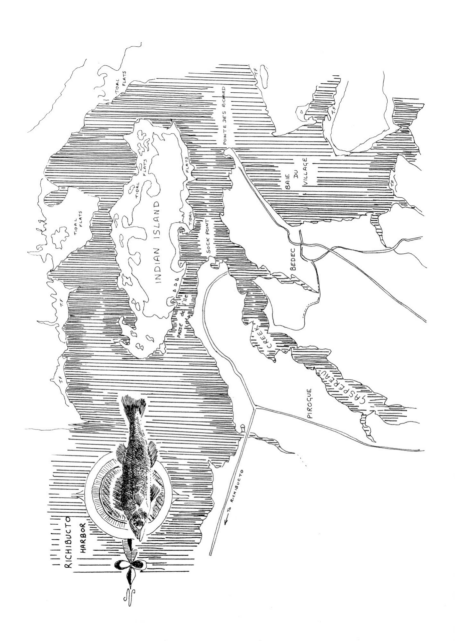

Chapter Nine

INDIAN ISLAND:
HOME OF THE RICHIBUCTOS

"The Indian does well to remain Indian."
 — Henry David Thoreau

"This island, the birthplace of the Richibuctos, is ours. It has been paid for by the lives of our ancestors who all lie buried here. Our future lies in preserving our past."
 — Chief Beter Barlow

Every major bay and stretch of Maritime coastline was once dominated by islands sacred to our native people. Each of these islands was a gathering place where the Micmacs, the Malecites or the Passamaquoddies of the region held special ceremonies and conducted burial rites. Islands set aside for these purposes tended to be small — rarely more than two miles long, oval in shape, and extraordinarily lovely. The site was important since it was here that every member of the tribe would take his final rest. For generations the first people of this land slept undistrubed beneath the tall trees of their sacred islands, lulled by the music of the nearby sea, free to commune with the spirits of nature which had ruled their lives.

The coming of white settlers changed all this. They often found the strategically-located offshore islands best for their purposes as well — purposes generally at odds with those of the Indians. What happened to 'Indian' Island in the Bay of

109

YOU ARE NOW ENTERING INDIAN ISLAND

THE CHIEF IN INDIAN ISLAND IS A BARLOW
THE FIRST COUNCILLOR IS A BARLOW

THE SECOND COUNCILLOR IS A BARLOW
THE MANAGER IS A BARLOW

THE SPOKESMAN IS A BARLOW
THE COOK, DEW IS A BARLOW

PLEASE DRIVE CAREFULLY BECAUSE THE
PERSON YOU WILL HIT WILL BE A BARLOW

Fundy (Charlotte County) — one of New Brunswick's eight
'Indian' islands — in its first hundred years of white settlement
was in many ways typical of the fate of other Indian islands in
the Maritimes.

* * * * * * * * * *

In 1760 James Chaffey, an energetic and ambitious
Englishman, visited the tiny (mile long) island. This treed and
pristine place which the Indians called 'little Jeganagoose'
seemed just the spot he had been looking for. It was central,
fertile and beautiful — from Chaffey's point of view the ideal
headquarters for a fur trading venture! Chaffey wasted little
time getting started. In short order he had built a house on the
island which is often referred to as the first on Passamaquoddy
Bay, despite the fact that an Acadian family had built a house
on the island as early as 1704. Chaffey's house, however, was
on a grander scale and was to become the centre of his trading
empire. From the beginning Chaffey asserted his strong will
over the Indians. The Passamaquoddies watched with awe the
takeover of their territory by this dynamic and
incomprehensible stranger.

Chaffey prospered, and because of him Indian Island
grew to be a trading centre with as many as twelve schooners at
one time lying at anchor offshore, waiting to load or unload
cargo. Gradually the island drew other businessmen. One of
these was a man called Goldsmith whose business involved
boiling sea water to extract salt. In fueling his fires for this
enterprise, Goldsmith managed to denude the island of all its
magnificent trees.

Now bare and bleak, the once-lovely and sacred island
had been defiled. No longer was it a suitable resting place for
'The People' — living or dead. The Indians, puzzled by the
influx of white settlers to the neighboring islands where they
had camped all their lives, like their fathers before them,
gradually withdrew into unfamiliar territory where many of
them perished quietly. In 1850 Moses Perley, on a government
mission to assess the potential of the Grand Manan fisheries,
noted in passing a few Indians camped on the rugged western
coast of Grand Manan and fishing just off shore. After that
there seems to be no mention of the island Passamaquoddies.

The Fundy fogs seem to have engulfed them forever.
For the newcomers to the Fundy isles, 'Indian' Island continued to be the logical central meeting place. Just like the Indians, the settlers congregated here to enact rites, albeit, rites incomprehensible to the native people — voting on election day, celebrating militia day, and exchanging songs, yarns and drinks. Although the new islanders continued to refer to their meeting place as 'Indian Island,' all that remained of the Indians' centuries-old occupation were a few fading patterns beaten into the earth.

* * * * * * * * * *

Of the 'Indian' islands still recorded on contemporary maps of the Maritime Provinces, the one which today most closely resembles descriptions of ideal 'Indian' islands in their original, unspoiled state is Indian Island in Richibucto Harbor. This island, sometimes referred to as Richibucto Island, has from time immemorial been sacred to the Richibuctos, a dominant band of Micmac or salt water Indians whose territory once extended along the Atlantic coast from the Gulf of Saint Lawrence to the present city of Boston. The Richibuctos had a village at the southern tip of this island both before and after the Fench 'discovered' the island in the seventeenth century. Although all traces of this village have long since vanished, the ceremonial markings on the earth near the original settlement are still visible.
Despite the Indians' continuous presence on or near this site over the centuries, the ownership of the island has been disputed since the seventeenth century when small portions of it were meted out to various French grantees. Yet even government officials have been troubled by the problem of ownership here, and have been aware of the island's importance to the Indians. This awareness has been underlined by the observations of the perspicacious Moses Perley in his reports on Indian affairs in the 1840's. In a communiqué composed for his superior, dated October 21, 1847, Mr. Perley remarked: "The Indians are stated to have a great fondness for Richibucto Island where they have held their annual festival on Saint Anne's day (26 July)." He recommended a quick and final solution to the dispute over the island, whereby the

Indians would acquire clear title to it. Throughout his reports, Mr. Perley's admiration for the Richibuctos and their quality of life is clearly evinced through such comments as: "The Richibuctos are athletic men and noted for their industry." Mr. Perley's recommendations about Indian Island, as about a number of other matters connected with Indian affairs in New Brunswick, met with official displeasure. For instance, in July 1848 (less than a year after his report on Indian Island) he received a reprimand from a government official, J.S. Saunders, part of which read: "...I am directed to inform you that your interference with Indian Affairs when you have not direct authority from the government is calculated to produce dissatisfaction among many of the Indians and to embarrass the Government in their endeavors to carry out the wishes of the Legislature."

Shortly after this missive was sent, Mr. Perley was directed to turn his attention from the Indians to the state of the fisheries on Grand Manan. Yet in retrospect the wisdom of Moses Perley's recommendations concerning the Indians of New Brunswick seems obvious. As W.D. Hamilton and W.A. Spray, professors of the University of New Brunswick's recently inaugurated Indian Studies Program, remarked: "Had Moses Perley's generally enlightened recommendations been followed in the 1840's, perhaps the new Brunswick Indians would have had less cause for dissatisfaction with the century that followed."

This disputed island, the Richibuctos' traditional rallying place, is densely wooded. Like Shediac Island, it lies low in- the water and is essentially an overgrown sand bar barely two miles long, with tidal flats occupying much of the outer side of the island. However, unlike Shediac Island, Indian Island is protected from blustery weather in the Northumberland Straits by a long sand dune protruding from the mainland. The inner side of the island runs parallel to the mainland point of land on which the Richibucto Indians of the Indian Island band have their permanent dwellings. The channel between mainland and island here is so narrow that the distance separating the two seems often little more than a stone's throw. This channel is only just wide enough and deep enough to deter the casual visitor from crossing to the island to inspect the enchanting wigwams which stand at widely spaced intervals along the shore just at the entrance to the woods.

This is likely just as well since from time to time intruders who have ventured into the Indians' sacred preserves with the persistent intention of violating them in some way have been visited with afflictions as strange and terrible as any recorded in Homeric legends. One would almost think that some powerful unseen force guards this tiny island and its surrounding waters on whose bounty 'The People' have always depended.

One of those who seems most recently to have incurred the wrath of the island spirits was, according to the story, a man who rented a light plane so that he could fly over the island and take aerial photographs with a view to taking the island from the Indians. Since the day was clear and sunny, he apparently flew back and forth over the island many times filming it from every angle through the most sophisticated lenses. However, we are told that he never saw the pictures he took. Shortly after his flight, his sight began to fail, and before the pictures had been developed he was absolutely blind.

Another story of seeming retribution concerns a man who crossed the river to dig clams on Indian land. He was asked to leave because there were barely enough clams for the Indians themselves, who had for some time been digging them sparingly so as not to deplete this favorite resource.

"Oh," the intruder is supposed to have replied when asked to stop digging. "I can't. I have to dig here since there are no clams left on my side of the river."

With the conversation closed in this manner, he continued to dig, filling bucket after bucket and loading them into his boat. The next day he returned and did the same. The Indians were heartsick, but felt there was nothing they could do. Force was out of the question. There chief would not permit it.

The third day they could not bear to return to watch the greedy intruder dig, so they were not among the first to learn that his boat had apparently capsized and that he had drowned.

Still, with his death the Indians were not free of intruders, for within a week of the first clam digger's death, a second digger had appeared. This man, the son of the first, was no more easily deterred than his father. After finding him just as impossible to convince, the Indians again withdrew sadly. However, the spirits of the waters must have been strongly offended, for within several days the son was found dead in his bed, apparently of a heart attack.

After hearing such tales one might well wonder about the powers and attitudes of the man who controls Indian Island. A first insight into the chief's character — apart from glowing newspaper reports, both local and international — was the comment of one of his neighbors, an Acadian fisherman on the wharf at Richibucto: "The chief, Peter Barlow, is a very good fellow.... He keeps everyone out there in line... In fact," he added with a twinkle in his eye, "it's too bad we don't have someone like him right here in Richibucto!"

Peter Barlow is a man whose response to life has remained enthusiastic and positive. He clearly enjoys his position as chief, despite the fact that it is, by his own admission, a twenty-four hour, three hundred and sixty-five day a year undertaking. He must have served his people well since he has been elected as well as hereditary chief for forty-eight years — since he was fifteen. He has indeed held on to his position longer than any of the other nearly five hundred contemporary Canadian Indian chiefs.

Chief Barlow and his wife live on an idyllic tract of land within sight of the sea and his beloved island. On his home ground he is surrounded by Barlows as the plaque at the entrance to Indian Island reservation proclaims:

YOU ARE NOW ENTERING INDIAN ISLAND
THE CHIEF OF INDIAN ISLAND IS A BARLOW
THE FIRST COUNCILLOR IS A BARLOW
THE SECOND COUNCILLOR IS A BARLOW
THE MANAGER IS A BARLOW
THE COM. DAV. IS A BARLOW
PLEASE DRIVE CAREFULLY BECAUSE THE
PERSON YOU WILL HIT WILL BE A BARLOW

Like the above, all signs on the reservation are in English, as are written communications with the outside world. However, in some households, the chief's for instance, the Micmac language is often spoken. Yet, some of the Barlows' grandchildren who attended English schools do not understand more than a handful of Indian words. This is a pity since linguistic authorities of the past have commented enthusiastically on the poetic and musical qualities of the Micmac language, much as Grey Owl rhapsodized about the expressive possibilities of the Ojibway tongue. Reverend Silas Rand, an accomplished Nova Scotia-born linguist who lived for forty years among the Micmacs, said of their language: "Do you ask which is my favorite language? Micmac. Why? Because it is one of the most marvellous of all languages, ancient or modern — marvellous in its construction, in its regularity, in its fulness."[1] He cited systematically comparisons between the Micmac language and Greek and Latin. More than three hundred of the Micmac words he lists have their classical counterparts. Some of the most obvious are:

MICMAC	ENGLISH	GREEK
Padoos	boy	Paidos
Come	a harbour	Come
Ekai	I am going	Eko
Oolk	boat	Olkas
Keloos	good	Kalos
Oonuks	wings	Onux

MICMAC	ENGLISH	LATIN
Ait	he says	Ait
Jun	child	Junenis
Agwith	water	Aqua
Qweentum	I ask	Quaero

Face to face with such linguistic similarities, what is one to think? What contact could the Micmacs have had with Latin and Greek long before recorded history? What never-recorded voyages to our shores could have taken place before those of Cartier, Champlain and Nicholas Denys to make such linguistic similarities possible?

Whereas one is stranded high and dry without clues about the apparent linguistic impact of the Greeks and Romans on the Micmacs, the influence of the French on the

Micmac language poses no such mysteries. The appearance of the French explorers bearing new implements and ideas simply made the coining of additional words necessary for the Indians. For instance, after spotting (perhaps at one of Denys' more permanent encampments) a European type of dwelling — a hitherto unheard of structure with four straight walls set upright to form a square or a rectangle and topped with a roof, they were clearly at a loss to describe this foreign architecture precisely by using their word for their own homes — 'wigwom'. Consequently, they came up with the more explicit descriptive word, 'Wenjeegwom' (French wigwom)! By the time the Micmacs learned that not only the French, but the English and other 'foreign' peoples as well, lived in the unusually shaped dwellings, the word was too firmly entrenched by usage to be altered. Thus, ironically, today even their own homes fall into the category of 'French wigwoms'!

Although even six or seven years ago one could perhaps have assumed that the Micmac language and culture would soon be extinct, there are signs of a revival of interest and pride in being Indian. This is strongly manifest in the names of the chief's four youngest grandchildren. They have indigenous Micmac names — Gooo (forest), Nibooktuk (pine), Oonig (fog). The baby has been named after the legendary American chief, Geronimo!

Another favorite and symbolic name which the chief has given another of his grandchildren (as well as a road on the Indian Island Reseveration) is 'Wilder'. This name is dear to him partly because of the gratitude he feels he owes Dr. Wilder Penfield, the great Canadian neurosurgeon whom he credits with saving the life of his son, Second Peter, and partly because of the therapeutic wilderness images which this word evokes. After all, the chief obviously subscribes to the ancient Indian beliefs which are best verbalized in Thoreau's epigramatic statements, such as "In Wilderness is the preservation of the World" and "From the wilderness come the barks and tonics which heal mankind".

And if Chief Peter Barlow and his band should fail to get back their island, what will happen to it? After reading an advertisement for souvenir centimeters of another Maritime Indian Island, one cannot help but fear tht the same obscene fate might await the island birthplace of Richibuctos:

118.

In fulfilling such traditional functions as naming his progeny and the places in his domain, and in his role as representative and figurehead of his people, the chief is rather like a reigning monarch. Like any king, he sits periodically for his portrait which is looked forward to and acclaimed both by his entourage and by his outside admirers.

However, to continue to hold office, the modern chief must cope with problems which his predecessors must never have imagined in their worst nightmares: the increasing demands of women for recognition, the culturally-destructive intrusions of the media (particularly television), encroachments on wild land, busing children to schools where teachers do not understand traditional ways or values, depletion and pollution of traditional fishing grounds — in a nutshell, the problems which beset most of the world's leaders in our times. Chief Barlow deals with these and other issues as best he can — often successfully — with the easy-going good temper he shares with many other maritimers.

As for intrusions on Indian Island, when they seemed so pressing in the seventies, the chief in 1975 in a grand public gesture crossed formally to the island to call attention to past injustices and government lethargy concerning Indian rights to the island. Chief Barlow underlined the significance of Indian Island for the ongoing life of his people: "This island, the birthplace of the Richibuctos, is ours. It has been paid for by the lives of our ancestors who lie buried here. Our future lies in preserving and building on our past."

1. Rand, Silas T., "Introduction", *Legends of the Micmacs*, p. xvii.

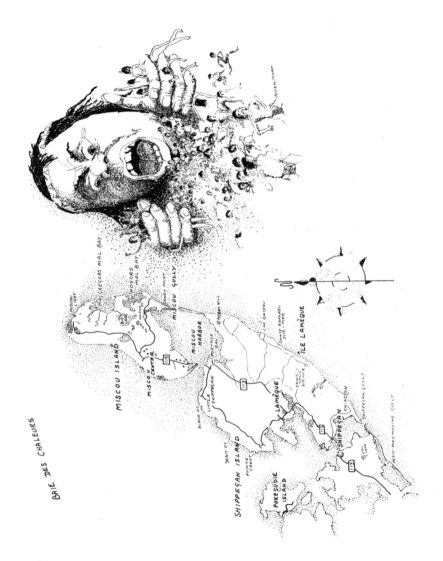

BAIE DES CHALEURS

MISCOU ISLAND

SHIPPEGAN ISLAND

POKESUDIE ISLAND

LAMÈQUE

SHIPPEGAN

ÎLE LAMÈQUE

Chapter Ten

MISCOU ISLAND:
ITS FISHERMEN AND MISSIONARIES
ITS MONSTER AND GHOST SHIP

A wooden lighthouse, reckoned to be perhaps the oldest of the original lighthouses built along the Northumberland Straits, still stands sentinel at Miscou Point on the historic and enchanted island which is so strategically situated at the northern end of the straits and the entrance to the Bay of Chaleur. Built in 1856, this lighthouse has over the years provided direction for brigs and schooners as well as for their motorpowered successors, although it seems to have been of no use to the mysterious ghost ships which have been reported burning and foundering off Miscou just as often in the last century and one half as in the two and one half preceding centuries of this island's extraordinary history.

This lighthouse was constructed relatively late in the four hundred years of Miscou's recorded history. Few places in Canada can boast of having records which go back so far into the past (only Cape Sable Island, the LaHave Islands and Scatarie Island are possible island contenders) — and even fewer have had such varied and unusual visitors and residents in fact the folklore. Cartier and Chaplain were among the earliest and most famous visitors; Nicholas Denys and the Jesuit fathers among the first dedicated visionaries; the "Gougou," resident sea monster, perhaps the largest, fiercest

122

and most exotic monster on record since the Homeric legends.

Despite its remarkable past, contemporary Miscou seems at first glance unremarkable. It has neither the lush growth nor the dreamy pastoral charm of other Northumberland Strait islands such as Pictou, Port Hood, or Cocagne, nor does it have the stark beauty of some of the rockbound islands off Nova Scotia's eastern, southern and Fundy coasts. Miscou sits low in the water — indeed it is gradually being inundated — and is ringed with fine sandy beaches. Almost half the island has always been unfit for human habitation (though a paradise for water birds, hunters and berry pickers) because of numerous bogs and ponds. The island's name is, in fact, derived from the Micmac word 'M'susqu,' meaning "low or boggy ground." The habitable portion is meadowland or sparsely-treed woodland. The trees, however, seem never to have recovered from a fire which, according to Denys' account, ravaged the island in the seventeenth century when a gunner who was getting his powder dry on the island accidentally exploded it while lighting his pipe.

The island houses appear to be comfortable and the churches well-maintained and suitable for their congregations, but none of the buildings now standing dates back before the nineteenth century. The Indians, the fishermen of many nationalities, the traders, the explorers, the missionaries — all those who occupied Miscou before the final resettlement of the island in 1815 — disappeared without leaving much evidence of their occupation. Unfortunately, nothing remains of the Jesuit chapel, built during the missionaries' sojourn on the island between 1635 and 1662, save the broken remnants of a handmade chalice unearthed several years ago near the grass-covered foundation of the ancient church. Of the elaborate seigneurie, complete with fruit trees, which Nicholas Denys established for himself in 1652 on the harbour, on Shippagan Island just opposite the mission, nothing remains either except a basement.

Over the years, visitors' and residents' reactions to Miscou have varied tremendously. About no other island have responses been so disparate. For some, Miscou has seemed one of the most idyllic spots on earth; for others, one of the bleakest. The following remarks, the first by the famous historian, W.F. Ganong (1906); the second by a Jesuit priest (1947), represent both points of view. Even today these opposing viewpoints have their supporters. A part of Ganong's eulogy reads:

> Miscou; — ever to me an island of charm. For I find it goodly in clime and fair to see; storied of old and ancient today; strange in form and forever in change; haunt of wild life and home of kind men; our Ultima Thule, great for the student and seeker of rest.
>
> (*History of Miscou*)

The Jesuit account begins with the following statement:

> The island of Miskou, about seven leagues (twenty-eight kilometers) around the perimeter, is situated in the Gulf of Saint Lawrence...; the soil is not good, the water is not wholesome, the trees are neither so tall nor so beautiful as on the mainland.... (*Relations des Jésuites*)

The Jesuit's disparaging tone is not difficult to understand when one learns more about the priests' lives on Miscou early in the seventeenth century. Those who were sent to the island, with the exception of Father André Richard and Father de Lyonne, were not robust men. Scholarly and ascetic, dedicated and faithful to their last breath, they seemed as surely doomed to die, victims of an alien environment, as were their brothers, martyred by the Iroquois in Upper Canada. And from all accounts, the sufferings of Miscou's pioneer clerics were at least as drawn out and horrible as the dramatic tortures undergone by more famous martyrs.

Winter, often harsh on Miscou, was the season to be dreaded. Ice on the Gulf brought an end to the comings and goings of the boats which all summer had plied regularly between Quebec and the island. The little settlement whose bountiful harvest of fish and skins contributed so much to both new and old world prosperity was on its own from November to May. As had happened with earlier settlements on Miscou during Champlain's time, nearly everyone left the island for the winter, so that only a handful remained behind — chiefly to look after fishing gear which would be needed the following summer. Champlain, obviously appalled by the difficulties of life on Miscou in this season, recorded how in the terrible winter of 1627 eight feet of snow fell on the island between November and the end of April, wiping out the garrison left there.

The Jesuits did not abandon their flock during the winter, although the difficult environment, together with the attitudes of some of their parishioners, would have made most ordinary men acknowledge defeat and leave after a first encounter. The missionaries were constantly reminded of the fact that their parishioners, particularly their recent Indian converts, needed frequent manifestations of benign divine intervention in practical matters to maintain their faith and that their main focus was, of necessity, simply physical survival.

That the missionaries understood the Indians' conflicts between religious commitment and practical necessity is evident in the following story which an early Miscou priest related. One Christmas Eve the priests were waiting to celebrate midnight mass. Two Indians set out for the chapel, but three leagues (twelve kilometers) from their cabin they encountered bear tracks. Since their houses were 'already haunted by the spectre of famine,' they were tempted to go hunting rather than attend church. New snow was fast covering the tracks, so there was no time to waste. Yet despite the strong temptation and their pressing need, the Indians did eventually decide to forego the hunt and fulfil their religious duties first, as they had promised. Later, returning home from church, they again encountered fresh tracks, and this time they followed the tracks and killed the bear, thus providing themselves and their families with food for many days. These Indians were, we are told, once more strongly confirmed in their faith, but one wonders, just as the priest who recounted the story perhaps did, just how they might have reacted if they had not got that bear.

Before the missionaries came to Miscou, the "Gougou" terrorized the native people there. The Indians had told Champlain that the "Gougou" was an evil monster who dominated the island and the surrounding ocean. It appeared as a woman, they said, a being so huge that the tops of the masts on Champlain's ship would not come up to her waist. Indeed, the whole ship would vanish in her pouch, they said. In this pouch, they recounted, the creature stored the people she caught and later devoured them at leisure. Indeed, the "Gougou" ate many Indians regularly, the Native People told Champlain seriously.

This monster was also supposed to make strange and horrible noises near the island. Not only the native people, but also "Le sieur Prévert de Saint-Malo" who had sailed by Miscou with many Indians aboard during his search for minerals, told Champlain about passing near the dwelling of this frightful beast, where all those on board his vessel heard the strange whistling noises which it made. Perhaps they merely heard the bubbling of the unusual fresh water fountain which Denys discovered welling up in mid ocean several hundred feet off the island — a fountain which, by the way, no longer exists.[1]

Whatever people saw and heard off Miscou, Champlain seemed unsure. He ended his speculations about the "Gougou" with this reflection: "I conclude that the island is home of some devil who torments them (the Indians) in this fashion." What Champlain did not say, and probably did not know, was that Micmac folklore has always favored evil giants (kookwés), many with cannibalistic propensities.[2]

Whether beast or devil, the "Gougou" was not spoken of after the Jesuit occupation of Miscou. There appear to be no accounts of its fearful doings after 1635. Thus, although the mission was not judged a success and was closed in 1662, the missionaries were perhaps more successful than they thought in exorcising the island's demons.

The disappearance of the "Gougou" did not, however, mean the end of strange and unexplained activity in the vicinity of Miscou. The weird phenomenon, the phantom ship, has been closely linked with this island throughout the years. This is understandable since Miscou is located between two favorite ship haunts — the Bay of Chaleur and the Northumberland Straits. The burning ship, sometimes seen at first as a ball of fire, has been sighted in ancient and modern times, in summer

126

and winter (even on the ice), before, during and after storms as well as in clear weather, during the day and at night. Some even say it is an evil omen, "le feu de mauvais temps," presaging disaster, as on June 5, 1914, when the ghost ship was seen twice before twenty Miscou fishermen perished at sea during a freak blizzard.

According to one version, Miscou's ghost ship dates from the beginning of the nineteenth century and is associated with the nefarious exploits of a certain Captain Craig who was, we are told, one of the most conniving and pitiless of pirates to pillage coastal settlements around the Bay of Chaleur. Like the earlier piratical tyrant of the inner reaches of the Bay, the notorious sixteenth century Portuguese Captain Corte-Real,[3] Captain Craig's favorite victims were in Indian settlements. Both pirates cynically got the Indians helplessly intoxicated so that they could make off with their most valuable possessions — especially the best animal pelts — and sometimes even the most attractive or prestigious of the natives.

Captain Craig, like many other captains who entered the Bay of Chaleur, was shrewd enough to realize that in certain parts of the Bay he would be safer with a local pilot, familiar with all its idiosyncrasies. Thus, like the merchant captains, he was in the habit of picking up a pilot from Miscou Island before proceeding into the Bay.

On this particular occasion, the Miscou pilot, following instructions, guided Captain Craig's sailing ship to the Indian settlement on the nearby coast then returned home to wait until he was needed to steer the ship out to sea again.

Several days later, when he had just begun to pilot the boat on its return trip through the most dangerous passage to the open sea, he thought he heard cries and groans coming from the hold. When these noises persisted, he insisted on the sails being lowered so that he could investigate the cause. To his dismay, the pilot found two young Indian girls bound hand and foot. Before agreeing to proceed further, he demanded that they be released. Although the captain and mate were most reluctant to free the girls, they could hardly refuse — unless they wished to jeopardize their ship and its precious cargo in such a precarious situation. Thus the girls were returned to their tribe and the ship began to move seaward once more under the direction of the Miscou pilot.

The Indian girls, however, had a premonition that the pirate ship was doomed. Although not displeased that retribution should be meted out to their captors, they suffered agonies at the thought that the man who had saved them would likely perish too.

As the girls had foreseen, the boat sank within minutes of leaving the shore, after striking Miscou Rock. All on board perished except the pilot who, because he was a strong swimmer, reached shore safely. Several months later he married the eldest of the Indian girls, and they are said to have lived a long and happy life together.

From the time of this shipwreck onwards, the pirate ship was often spotted off Miscou. Before its appearance, a powerful red light was seen to detach itself from Miscou Rock and skim over the surface of the Bay. Gradually this ball of fire took on the shape of a boat which in all its details was said to be clearly recognizable as Captain Craig's boat. It sailed toward shore, and then, within a hundred feet of the bank, it disappeared. The comings and goings of the burning ship over the years have been recorded, pondered over and investigated by local residents and by imported specialists[4] — all to no avail. No one has yet come up with a satisfactory or conclusive explanation.

Settlement on Miscou, as on sister island outposts such as Cape Sable, LaHave and Scatarie, was attempted at such an early period in this country's history because of the extraordinary promise of its fisheries. For more than four centuries Miscou islanders have been fishermen first and foremost.

Small wonder! Moses Perley in his 1852 *Report on the Fisheries* lists the varieties of fish found in abundance off Miscou at that time: salmon, halibut, trout, shad, sturgeon, mackerel, cod, ling, flounder, plaice, crab, sculpin, lobster, and shrimp. Schools of some of these fish, such as mackerel, were so prolific that they appeared alongside boats as "almost in a solid mass."[5] Huge numbers of fish were taken by the islanders themselves, by mainlanders and by visiting American fishermen. Mr. Perley, a conservationist long before such a role was fashionable, was obviously appalled by the widespread waste and mismanagement he observed. Everyone, he indicated, was to blame.

The Jersey houses which for so many years owned all the fishing stations on Miscou were troublesome, Mr. Perley stated, because they refused to "furnish salt, even to their best customers to cure herring, mackerel or any pickled fish; and they discouraged the catching and curing of all fish, except such as were dried and fit for the foreign markets."[6] Partly as a result of this practice, most of the fish (particularly herring and mackerel) were used as fertilizer: "It is thought that no more than one tenth of the fish they take are salted the remaining nine-tenth being put on the fields as manure."[7] Shrimps, brought on shore in large quantities "were turned out again as being of no use."[8] Furthermore, visiting American fishermen were often known to throw out one cargo of fish if a more lucrative one offered: "An American vessel fishing off Point Miscou and having on board nearly a full fare of cod, had found the mackerel in such extraordinary abundance, that the crew had thrown overboard one hundred and fifty quintals of green fish, in order to make room for mackerel, with which the vessel had been quickly filled up."[9]

Yet despite such waste, the Miscou fisheries were not noticeably depleted by the next century. 1916 was a record year. That was the year when a good fisherman could take in twenty-two hundred pounds of lobster in a single trip! (His pay for such a catch was a cent and one half a pound!)

Miscou's population has always depended on the ups and downs in the fisheries. When the fisheries thrived and the markets were strong, the population grew: when the catches diminished or the markets decreased, an exodus of island dwellers was sure to result.

Because settlements on this island were started so often over the years and then abandoned, paradoxically the permanent occupation (begun about 1815) was much later than on such islands as Brier, Grand Manan, Tancook and others which were settled for the first time in the late eighteenth century but were then tenaciously held on to by the descendents of these early immigrants.

Another paradoxical fact about Miscou's final settlement is that it was begun by Anglophones. Given its location and early history, one is at first greatly surprised to learn from so reliable a source as Ganong's "History of Miscou" that "of all the settlements of the North Shore of New Brunswick, this one alone owes the inauguration of its permanent settlement to the English rather than to the French." The place-names — 'Wilson's Point,' 'Miscou Harbour,' and 'Miscou Point' — attest to the continuing influence of the first Anglophone residents, as do the small protestant churches which are still so well maintained in both Miscou Harbour and Miscou Point.

However, in the last bid for settlement on Miscou, Francophone settlers soon arrived from many parts of "Acadie," from France, from Quebec and from the Island of Jersey. They put down roots in Grande Plaine, a village which had once before (from about 1719 to 1730) gained prominence in this island's history because of the amazing numbers of sea cows or walruses slaughtered there. The rapid extermination of these gentle creatures coincided with the demise of the settlement.[10]

The new Francophone settlers at Grande Plaine were fishermen like most of the earliest island residents and like their Anglophone neighbors. This final settlement at Grande Plaine flourished and grew so that soon several families moved inland to establish the community which is now known as Miscou Centre. Over the years the Francophone population has grown more quickly than the Anglophone, and now most of the island's population is French and is concentrated in Miscou Centre where there is a large Catholic church, a school and several stores.

The number of people on the island has fluctuated during this century as much as in the three preceding centuries. In 1906 W.F. Ganong recorded the island's population as between four and five hundred. This figure, he predicted (probably correctly) was the limit the land and surrounding sea could comfortably maintain. Yet because of a thriving fishery, the population grew until by 1947 it was three times Ganong's ideal number — about 1500. After this, with the closure of many fish plants, the numbers dwindled.

Like so many other offshore islands of the Maritime

Provinces, Miscou was to some extent affected by the general twentieth century trend away from island living — a trend which peaked in the early fifties. Whereas in this rapid exodus, such long-established island communities as those on Scatarie, Cape Negro, Cocagne, Heron, Shediac, Liscomb and McNutt's were deserted almost overnight, Miscou's colony shrank only gradually — and only toward Ganong's ideal population figure. By 1973 there were half as many residents as there had been in 1947: fifty-two families (seven hundred and forty-five people).

According to existing accounts,[11] most of those who now remained on the island were unlikely to be dislodged. They were tenacious in clinging to their island roots. One old man is supposed to have announced, "They won't get me out of here alive and make me go and live somewhere else in a shack. Deprived of the Gulf air, it would be better to die!" And down the road in Miscou Centre a ninety-year-old woman (in the spring of 1973) was out digging her garden, her left arm in a sling because she had broken her wrist toward the end of the winter. This woman, Annie Ward, was obviously cut from the same strong fabric as Christiania Davis, the Brier Island woman who had walked to Halifax and back to settle a land dispute.

Miscou residents have somehow managed to live with the main problem faced by all Northumberland Strait or Bay of Chaleur island residents — namely, unsafe ice (particularly during freeze-up and thaw), which can make crossing to the mainland such a hazardous undertaking. They obviously feel that their lifestyle is worth the risk. "A causeway from Miscou to Lamèque would change the pace of life here, in the winter especially," one man remarked. "It wouldn't be so tranquil here if this wasn't a *real* island. As things are now, you have to think ahead and lay in supplies for winter. Planning that far ahead makes for a different mentality than most people on the mainland have now."

But whether French or English, Catholic or Protestant, the island residents seem happy with their lot and on the whole pleased with one another. As an eighth-generation descendant of a Jersey fisherman remarked: "We are one big, happy family here. We all love the island and the sort of life it gives us. You must remember that living on an island means that everyone *has* to look out for his neighbor. That improves the quality of life!"

1. In 1906 W.F. Ganong went to the island and searched for this fountain, but was unable to find it.

2. See Rev. Silas T. Rand, *Legends of the Micmacs*, Longmans, Green and Co., New York and London, 1894 (reprinted 1971). One tale of a cannibalistic giant included in this book is "The History of Kitpooseagunow — A Tale of Ancient Times" 9 pp. 62-80 . Rand carefully transcribed such tales as this from the original oral tales. Rand was, by the way, a painstaking scholar and an extraordinary linguist who spent forty years working among the Micmacs and studying their language and culture — in a comparative context, it might be added. In the course of his studies, Rand mastered twelve languages (English, Latin, Greek, Hebrew, French, Italian, German, Spanish, Modern Greek, Micmac, Maliseet and Mohawk) and acquired great insight into their respective cultures.

3. For an account of Corte-Real's doings see Chapter XI.

4. The most extensive listing of material relating to the sightings and explanations (both scientific and folkloric) is in *Le Vaisseau Fantôme (Légende étiologique)* by Soeur Catherine Jolicoeur (Les Archives de Folklore, Les Presses de l'Université Laval, 1970).

5. Moses Perley, *Report on the Sea and River Fisheries*, of New Brunswick, Queen's Printer, Fredericton, 1852, p. 36. Even today Miscou has an unusual reputation connected with its abundant seafood. A brief commentary by Michael Camp in *The Telegraph-Journal* (January 31, 1984, p. 5) begins as follows: "If a strong northeast wind suddenly shifts to the northwest, chances are the current will wash hundreds of lobsters onto the beaches of this small island. If you're quick enough you can collect a pail-full or two for dinner."

6. *Ibid.*, p. 34. Perley also quotes a Mr. Wilson of the island, who states: "...the Jersey houses exact too large profits, and keep the fishers in poverty; they look only to one branch of fishing and discourage all others." (p. 36) Elsewhere in his report, Perley refers to the "absolute state of serfdom" of the Point Miscou fishermen because of the practices of the Jersey houses. (p. 39)

7. *Ibid.*, p. 34.

8. *Ibid.*, p. 37.

9. *Ibid.*, p. 36.

10. For a touching account of this period in Miscou's history see Louis Haché's novel. *Adieu P'tit Chipagan*, Editions d'Acadie Ltée, Moncton, N.B., 1979.

11. See Louis Haché, *Charmante Miscou*, Editions d'Acadie, Moncton, 1979, pp. 27 and 29. "on ne me sortira pas d'icitte vivant pour aller vivre ailleurs dans un shack, proteste un vieux Miscou. Privé de l'air du golfe, mieux vaut mourir!" (p. 27) Michael Camp in *The Telegraph-Journal* (January 31, 1984, p. 5) lists the population of Miscou Island as 1,100.

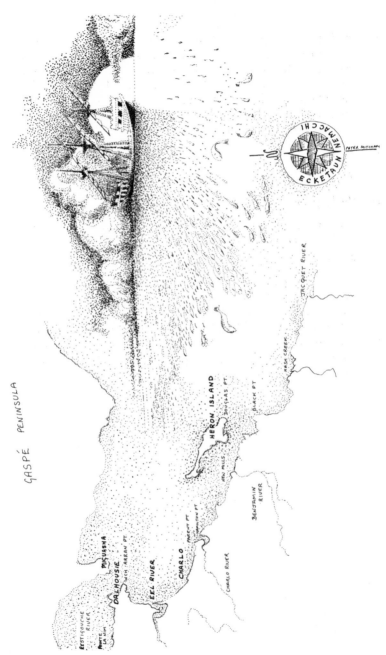

GASPÉ PENINSULA

RESTIGOUCHE RIVER
POINTE LA NIM
DALHOUSIE
MIGUASHA
INCH ARRAN PT.
EEL RIVER
CHARLO
INCH ARRAN PT.
BONAVENTURE PT.
CHARLO RIVER
PREROTT PT.
BENJAMIN RIVER
HERON ISLAND
NEW MILLS
DOUGLAS PT.
BLACK PT.
NASH CREEK
JACQUET RIVER

ECKETAUN
NEMACCHI
PETER MITCHELL

Chapter Eleven

HERON ISLAND:
ISLAND IN "THE SEA OF FISH"

The Bay of Chaleur possesses many advantages for the prosecution of the fisheries. The whole Bay may be considered one great harbour, as throughout its entire breadth and extent there is not a single rock, reef or shoal. During the summer it literally swarms with fish of every description known on the shores of British North America: and its ancient Indian name of "Ecketaun Nemacchi" — "The Sea of Fish" — well denotes its character.

— Moses Perley (1852)
Report on the Sea and River
Fisheries of New Brunswick

The most significant island in this "Sea of Fish" is Heron Island which lies between New Brunswick and the Gaspé coast where the Bay of Chaleur begins to narrow to meet the Restigouche River. This long and narrow island (about five miles by one mile or less) is roughly two miles off the New Brunswick coast and more than triple that distance from Quebec. Because of its protected location and excellent fishing, comparable for these reasons to the Northumberland Strait islands of Cocagne and Shediac, it seems an ideal habitat for herons who appear from earliest recorded times to have been associated with this island. The Indians too found this place greatly to their liking, as did white immigrants who eventually, like the herons and the Indians, settled here because of the excellent fishing and the shelter it afforded.

Settlers or visitors, whether French or English, have consistently kept the same name for the island. In the earliest Louisbourg records frequent brief references are made to voyages undertaken to 'La Baie des Chaleurs,' where 'l'île-aux Herons' was sighted; and late eighteenth-century accounts use the same spelling as the Louisbourg records when referring to the granting of this island — together with some of the nearby mainland, including the land on which the town of Carlo now stands — to l'Abbé Bourg, the first Acadian priest serving as missionary in the Bay of Chaleur region.

L'Abbé Bourg had this land pressed upon him in the 1780's as a reward for quelling an Indian uprising. Apparently only his timely intervention saved bloodshed. Several sources indicate that no other white man of this time possessed so extensive a knowledge of the Indian languages and customs or was able to establish so strong a rapport with the native people as l'Abbé Bourg. Ironically, however, although Sir Richard Hughes made a great fanfare, which resounded from Hughes' own residence in Halifax to the good Abbé's residence at Carleton (on the Gaspé across from Heron Island), trumpeting Bourg's accomplishment and his own delight in rewarding him, he never actually gave Bourg a deed to the land he seemed eager to confer on him. Bourg, moreover, who was by all accounts an unworldly man, appears to have been so concerned with attending to the spiritual welfare of his own people and the Indians under his jurisdiction that he had no time or energy to attend to lands on Heron Island.

It was not, therefore, until almost mid-nineteenth century that Heron Island was divided into twelve farms of unequal acreages stretching from shore to shore (north to south). These grants were taken up by Anglophone families. The chief occupation of these early settlers was fishing. As Moses Perley pointed out in his 1852 report: "There is excellent herring fishing around this island...lobster and sea trout are abundant." Nevertheless, Mr. Perley was upset by some of the inequalities governing the fishing here even at such an early date. The best fishing, he noted, was between the island and the New Brunswick mainland, and the lots already granted covered all the beaches, leaving no fishing stations available for newcomers.

Mr. Perley also quoted remarks made by a nearby mainland resident — a Mr. Harvey of Nash's Creek — that Americans should be allowed to "prosecute the fisheries (here), as they would teach the young men the latest and most approved modes of fishing, from ignorance of which they could not at present follow fishing profitably." That Mr. Perley did not protest against this viewpoint is surprising, given his knowledge of the difficulties resident fishermen of both Grand Manan and Miscou were having at this time with American interlopers and his perspicacity in spotting and calling attention to troublesome situations in advance.[1]

The American boats which fished so close to Miscou at this time and periodically entered the Bay of Chaleur were chiefly after cod, since the cod in the Bay was reputed to be of superior quality for shipping to the Mediterranean markets where it was much in demand. The Bay of Chaleur codfish were smaller than those caught elsewhere and were said to remain white and delicate even after being salted and dried.

Apart from its proximity to fine fishing, Heron Island has never had much in common with the larger neighboring island at the mouth of the Bay. On windswept Miscou, sparse evergreens struggle valiantly to hold their ground; on sheltered Heron, lush stands of cedars, poplars, birches, maples, as well as spruce and fir, reach upward and outward as they vie with one another for a place in the sun. Miscou's many bogs produce ground-hugging vegetation — pitcher plants, cranberries, and bakeapples: Heron's well-drained upland meadows generate shoulder-high grasses, multitudes of wild-flowers and raspberry bushes.

Heron Island, like Merigomish Island in Pictou County or Indian Island near Richibucto, was, understandably, a favorite haunt of the Micmacs. Here they dwelt under seeming ideal conditions until the coming of the white man caused them to abandon their beautiful island forever. The repercussions from this first clash between native people and European mariners proved disastrous for all concerned.

According to the story, the tragedy began in 1500 when an unscrupulous Portuguese adventurer, Gaspar Corte-Real, arrived in the Bay of Chaleur. Going ashore on the Gaspé coast opposite Heron Island, he and his crew piled a number of the chiefs with alcohol until they were hopelessly drunk — then took them prisoner and transported them to Europe to sell as slaves. Apparently not at all concerned that this treachery might boomerang.

Corte-Real returned to the Bay of Chaleur the following summer — this time to Heron Island. Since the Indians there seemed friendly, he assumed that either they knew nothing of the kidnapping which had taken place on the nearby Gaspé coast the previous summer — or that, if they knew, they did not care. Thus Corte-Real and his men, relaxing all vigilance, established themselves on the island and focused their attention on trading with the Indians. The Indians, however, were both cannier and more unforgiving than they seemed: they were merely biding their time for vengeance. One dark night when the Portuguese were asleep, the Indians stole into the Europeans' dwelling, murdering everyone except Corte-Real. For him they had devised a punishment in keeping with the crime he had committed against their people the preceding summer. Taking Corte-Real to a rock which was not submerged at low tide, they secured him to it and then abandoned him so that he would have a number of hours to reflect on his wicked life and approaching death before the tide rose over him.

Gaspar Corte-Real's death did not, however, put an end to unpleasant foreign intrusions, as no doubt the Indians had hoped, for the following summer (1502) Miguel Corte-Real, Gaspar's brother, came to find out what had happened to the captain and crew of the first trading vessel. Almost at once he spotted the *Caravel* moored, still intact, off the middle part of the island. As he saw no sign of life aboard, he sailed his own ship closer. Suddenly a large number of Indians shot out from shore in their canoes, clambered quickly aboard the vessel and at once massacred everyone in sight.

Seeing the fate of their fellows, the captain and surviving crew barricaded themselves in the cabin and below decks with all the weapons they could lay hands on. However, the *Caravel*, left untended, began to drift out to sea, and the sailors surmised that they were doomed. Before making a final rush on the Indians on deck, the Portuguese are supposed to have said a prayer which included the vengeful threat that, if they died, they would return to haunt the Bay of Chaleur for one thousand years.

During the final confrontation between the Portuguese and Indians the boat caught fire. Soon the sails and masts were ablaze and the gutted boat disappeared quickly beneath the waters of the Bay. Only one Indian survived to tell the story. We were told that even after all this the Indians were not left in peace because from this time on they kept seeing the burning ship bearing down upon them — particularly on the eve of a storm. Increasingly terrified by these strange and frequent reappearances of the lost ship, they abandoned Heron Island and went to live on the banks of the Restigouche River.

Ever since this time the burning ship has been spotted sailing up and down the Bay in all seasons of the year, though it is most often visible, some say, just before a storm. Hundreds of men, women and children have reported watching the vessel burn and at length sink into the sea.[2] Many contemporary viewers seem as puzzled and upset by the phenomenon as the Indians nearly five centuries ago are supposed to have been.

The settlers who finally became established on Heron Island seem to have been little troubled by ghosts of the past. Neither the restless spirits of the displaced Micmacs nor the vengeful spectres of the murdered Portuguese returned to mar the tranquility of their lives or the abundance of the harvests from land and sea. As former residents have been quick to emphasize: "Life on Heron Island was idyllic."

One man, Stanley LaPointe, who takes his family back every summer to camp on the beach below his family's former farmhouse, remarked: "Nowhere else has the same feeling of peace and plenty for me..... Even in the Depression with eleven kids in our family we always had enough. Like everyone else on the island, we had a good house, some animals, a great garden, berries galore, and lots of fish and firewood. Of course my father seemed almost rich at the time because, in addition to everything else that I have mentioned, he had two concurrent government jobs — lighthouse keeper and postmaster."

"Yes, we were lucky," he continued. "But now it's best that no one lives here. I'm glad the island is deserted. This way there's no way of it getting spoiled."

Mr. LaPointe did not elaborate on this last remark, but one only needs to see what has happened to nearby parts of the mainland — at Belledune, for example — to know what he means. Not so long ago that was once a lovely spot too. Because the whole Bay is, as Mr. Perley noted, such a fine and safe natural harbor of immense proportions, industries have seen the immediate advantages of locating here. By putting up ugly, sprawling concrete buildings, crowned with immense smokestacks and flanked by black-topped and machine-littered acres, they have already marred the scenery of one of the world's great natural beauty spots. Heron Island has fortunately been spared this sort of 'progress'.

However, like the rest of the Bay, the waters around Heron Island are slowly but surely being polluted by the many chemicals which industries all along the Bay spew daily into the once pure waters. Not only are the fish less numerous than they once were, but questions have been raised about the toxic levels of contaminants in the survivors.[3] Unless we can somehow manage to alter aspects of our development, "Echetaun Nemaachi", or "The Sea of Fish", will be nothing but a vague and haunting memory.

1. For a detailed account of the problems which the Miscou fishermen faced, see Perley's 1852 *Report on the Sea and River Fisheries of New Brunswick*, and, for a record of the difficulties in the Grand Manan fisheries, see Perley's 1850 *Report on the Fisheries of Grand Manan*.
    Actually, American boats had been coming to the Bay of Chaleur for the best part of the hundred years before Perley made his observations and wrote his report in 1852. This "Sea of Fish" was for years the primary destination of New England fishing boats and Jersey merchants alike. One of these merchants, Charles Robin, in his *Journal* (much of which is a day to day account of his business trips from Arichat, Isle Madame, Cape Breton to the Bay of Chaleur during the years 1767-1769) tells of the many schooners and whalers he observed each spring anchored between Canso and Isle Madame waiting for the drift ice to shift so that they could pass through into the Northumberland Straits. Once into the Straits, they

steered for Pictou Island, much as earlier fishermen along the Cape Breton coast had been guided by Scatarie Island as a landmark. However, unlike their European predecessors on the Cape Breton coast, there are no records of this new wave of transient fishermen either stopping on the island or coming to grief on its coast. Intent on reaching the "Sea of Fish", the only impediments once the ice had gone from the usually tranquil Northumberland Straits were sand bars off Cape Tormentine. Thus, reaching their favorite fishing grounds was usually not a difficult or dangerous undertaking.

2. The greatest number of accounts of these sightings are brought together in Soeur Catherine Jolicoeur's book, *Le Vaisseau fantôme, légend étiologique*, Les Presses de l'université Laval, Québec, 1970.

3. See Warner Troyer's *No Safe Place*, Clarke, Irwin, Toronto, 1977.

SOURCE MATERIAL

Below are listed some of the works consulted while researching this book. This list, however, represents only a small portion of the source material. For instance, particularly useful were manuscripts, letters, census reports, and maps available in various archives and libraries such as: Les Archives acadiennes (Université de Moncton), The Provincial Archives (Halifax and Fredericton), The Public Archives (Ottawa), The Louisbourg Archives, The Mount Allison Library, and the Legislative Library (Fredericton), McCulloch House Museum (Pictou), Shelburne District Museum. Much helpful information has also been provided by the Grand Manan Historical Society and the Chezzetcook Historical Society. As important as any of the above is all the information collected by word of mouth from scores of present and former island residents, from past and present lighthouse keepers and their families, and from fishermen — particularly those who have provided transportation to the various islands which are the subject of this book.

Selected Bibliography

Allen, C.R., *Illustrated Historical Atlas Pictou County*, Nova Scotia, J.H. Meacham and Co., 1879.

Barto, Martha Ford, Passamaquoddy, *Genealogies of West Isles Families*, Lingley Printing Co., Saint John, 1975.

Belliveau, John Edward, *Running Far In*, Lancelot, 1977.

Bollan, William, *The Importance and Advantage of Cape Breton*, New York, Johnson Reprint Corp., 1966. (First published in 1746).

Cape Breton Magazine, no. 14, Aug., 1976.

Chabert, M. de, *Voyage fait par ordre du roi en 1750 et 1751 dans l'Amérique Septentrionale*, Johnson Reprint Corporation, Mouton and Co., N.Y., 1966.

Champlain, Samuel de, *The Works of Samuel de Champlain*, 6 vols. The Champlain Society, Toronto, 1922. (French, with English translation and notes).

Day, Frank Parker, *Rockbound*, University of Toronto Press, Toronto, Buffalo, London, 1973. (First printed 1928).

D'Entremont, Clarence-Joseph, *Histoire du Cap-Sable de l'an mil au traité de Paris*, Hébert Publications, Eunice, Louisiana, 1981, 5 vols.

Nicholas Denys, Sa vie et son oeuvre, L'Imprimerie Lescarbot Ltée, Yarmouth, 1982.

Denys, Nicholas, *The Description and Natural History of the Coasts of North America* (Acadia), The Champlain Society, Toronto, 1908. (Original French text, together with translation and notes by W.F. Ganong.)

Desbrisay, Mather Byles, *History of the County of Lunenburg*, 2nd ed., W. Briggs, Toronto, 1895.

Faucher de Saint Maurice, Henri-Edouard, *Promenades dans le Golfe Saint-Laurent*, Montréal, 1881.

Fergusson, Charles Bruce, *Place Names of Nova Scotia*, Mika, 1975 (reprint).

Ganong, W.F., "The History of Miscou," *Acadiensis*, 1906.

Grand Manan Historian, Vol. 1-XXI, Grand Manan, New Brunswick.

Haché, Louis, *Charmante Miscou*, Editions d'Acadie Ltée., Moncton, N.B., 1974.

Adieu, P'tit Chipagan, Editions d'Acadie Ltée., Moncton, N.B., 1979.

Haliburton, Thomas Chandler, *An Historical and Statistical Account of Nova Scotia*, (2 vols.), Halifax, 1829.

Hamilton, W.D. and Spray, W.A., *Source Materials Relating to the New Brunswick Indians*, Hamray Books, Fredericton, 1977.

Holland's Description of Cape Breton Island, Compiled by D.C. Harvey, Public Archives of Nova Scotia, 1935.

Howe, Joseph, *Travel Sketches of Nova Scotia*, Halifax, 1928.

Inventaire General des Sources Documentaire sur les Acadiens, Le Centre d'études acadiennes, Université de Moncton, Editions d'Acadie, 1975.

Jolicoeur, Sr Catherine, *Le Vaisseau fantôme, légende étiologique*, Les Presses de l'Université Laval, 1970.

Lockwood, Anthony, *A Brief Description of Nova Scotia*, 1818.

Lorimer, John G., *History of the Islands and Islets in the Bay of Fundy*, Saint Croix Courrier, St. Stephen, 1876.

MacLaren, M.M., *Chetigne Island*, Reprinted by Chezzetcook Historical Society, 1980. (First published 1916.)

Martin, Robert Montgomery, *History of Nova Scotia*, Whittaker and Co., London, 1837.

McLennan, J.S., *Louisbourg*, The Book Room, Halifax, 1979. (First published by Macmillan in 1918.)

Melançon, Abbé Arthur, *Vie de l'Abbé Bourg, premier prêtre acadien*, Le 'Chez Nous,' Rimouski, 1921.

Murdoch, Beamish, *A History of Nova Scotia or Acadie*, James Barnes, Halifax, Vol. I — 1865, Vol. II — 1966.

Perley, Moses, *Report on the Sea and River Fisheries of New Brunswick*, Queen's Printer, Fredericton, 1852.

Rand, Silas T., *Legends of the Micmacs*, Longmans, Green & Co., New York and London, 1894.

Relations des Jésuits, (Tome 4 (1647-1655), Editions du Jour, Montréal, 1972.

Robin, Charles, *Journal of Charles Robin* (1767-1787), Public Archives, Ottawa.

Savoie, Francis, *L'Ile de Lamèque* Editions d'Acadie Ltée, Moncton, N.B., 1981.

Slocum, Joshua, *The Voyages of Joshua Slocum*, Collected and introduced by Walter Magnes Teller, New Brunswick, N.J., Rutgers University Press, 1958.

Stephens, David E., *Lighthouses of Nova Scotia*, Lancelot Press, Windsor, Nova Scotia.

Troyer, Warner, *No Safe Place*, Clarke, Irwin, Toronto, 1977.

Uniake, Richard John, *Sketches of Cape Breton*, Public Archives of Nova Scotia, ed., by C. Bruce Fergusson, Halifax, 1958.

Wilson, Beckles, *The Life and Letters of James Wolfe*, Heinemann, London, 1909.

DATE DUE
